Starting, Strengthening, and Managing Institutional Repositories:

A How-To-Do-It Manual®

Jonathan A. Nabe

HOW-TO-DO-IT MANUALS®

NUMBER 169

Neal-Schuman Publishers, Inc.

New York London

Published by Neal-Schuman Publishers, Inc.
100 William St., Suite 2004
New York, NY 10038

Printed and bound in the United States of America.

The paper used in this publication meets the minimum requirements of American National Standard for Information Sciences—Permanence of Paper for Printed Library Materials, ANSI Z39.48-1992.

Library of Congress Cataloging-in-Publication Data

Nabe, Jonathan A., 1966-
Starting, strengthening, and managing institutional repositories : a how-to-do-it-manual / Jonathan A. Nabe.
p. cm. — (How-to-do-it manuals ; no. 169)
Includes bibliographical references and index.
ISBN 978-1-55570-689-0 (alk. paper)
1. Institutional repositories—Administration. 2. Institutional repositories—United States—Case studies. I. Title.

ZA4081.86.N33 2010
025.04068—dc22

2009035176

For D.
For Everything

Contents

Preface

If you have assumed the mantle of an institutional repository (IR) manager, strap yourself in for the ride of your life. The highs will be higher than whatever else you have experienced in your work life, and the lows will have you ready to drop the whole thing into somebody else's lap. Opportunities for interacting with researchers and other content creators will be unprecedented—as will the delays and obstacles you will encounter when it comes time for those individuals to actually participate. The ability to meet a true need on the part of a faculty member or student to share work with colleagues and peers, and the gratefulness they will show when you provide them the means, can bring immense job satisfaction and is not something most librarians have the luck to experience. But, the echoes of that satisfaction will fade under the monotony of submitting document after document or reviewing endless metadata. You will have the chance to engage in pressing issues of scholarly communication, at all levels within your institution, and be presented with vital opportunities to educate everyone who participates in the information-sharing process about the economic, political, and social issues surrounding that process. Unfortunately, much of the audience will tune you out before you even begin. It is, unquestionably, a job of ups and downs. But it is a crucial one for the profession and for scholarly communication.

How This Book Can Help

Starting, Strengthening, and Managing Institutional Repositories: A How-To-Do-It Manual is written for anyone responsible for creating, developing, and maintaining an IR. It covers the essential components in this process, and it serves as a one-stop source for all of the information needed to adequately address each of these components. The book grew out of the author's experience starting IRs at two institutions, and the frustration at not having a resource at hand that comprehensively addressed the issues which arose during the process. This manual is designed to fill that gap.

Although the book can be read straight through and is presented in sequential order of planning and implementation procedures, it can also be consulted as needed. It is intended as a practical manual, not a theoretical framework, and will help in making specific decisions about starting and managing a repository. A repository coordinator is likely to be faced with challenges primarily in two areas: management and collection development. Management includes issues of staffing, budgeting, platform selection, and policy development. Each of these is covered in depth here. Solutions to the pressing issues of collection development, marketing, recruitment, and increasing use are also covered extensively. Indeed, because collection development is the area where IRs can be said to have struggled the most, half of the book is devoted to remedying the insufficient coverage the topic has received elsewhere.

Part I details each of the essential aspects in developing a successful IR. Chapter 1 addresses the issue of the role librarians should take in the implementation of IRs. Chapter 2 lays out the issues associated with the costs of IRs, in terms of budgeting and staffing, and touches on potential funding mechanisms. Chapter 3 describes the different types of platforms available, their pros and cons, and how to choose the right one for your institution. Chapter 4 covers policy writing, which is never exciting, but its value is often clear down the road, and it needs to be done right from the start. Preservation policies and issues are also discussed. It is important to hit the ground running, so, even before your IR is established, you need to have a marketing plan in place. Chapter 5 describes proven marketing techniques for attracting the interest of potential supporters and contributors. Marketing just whets the appetite, so Chapter 6 details methods of sustaining interest in your IR and continuing to grow the collection. Because copyright can have a significant impact on submissions, an understanding of what is and what is not allowed—and how to find out—is presented. Finally, techniques for increasing outside use of your IR are examined. And you will want to—even if you don't have to—assess the success of your IR (if nothing else, to see if it warrants further resources). Use of an IR is the primary method of assessment, and this topic is covered in Chapter 7.

Part II provides testimonials from the pros—coordinators by whatever title. In a series of success studies, real experiences from real people show how the principles described in Part I have been applied successfully. Shared access is a driving motivation for the development of IRs, and those involved in their development and management tend to have a philosophical commitment to that ideal. This ideological commitment means that there has been a great deal of sharing among IR coordinators, and every repository owes something to every other repository. This is true whether the platform is commercial or open source, whether the institution is large or small, public or private. Thus, the success studies in Part II provide a representative sample of all of these variations; each one of them will have something to teach, regardless of your own institutional setting. The IR staff at Cornell's Industrial and Labor Relations School details the marketing and outreach techniques employed to create their successful repository. At Colorado State University, the in-depth analysis used to arrive at the choice of platform is provided. There are different issues for smaller schools involved in IR support, and the case study from Macalester College raises and addresses those issues. Many institutions are transforming IRs into full publication systems, and the University of Illinois' IDEALS provides one such account. Texas State's experience clearly illustrates the importance of developing multiple marketing strategies, and the University of New Mexico shows the value of having a flexible policy toward different content types. Finally, the example of the University of Nebraska exemplifies the importance of having adequate and appropriate staffing in the pursuit of repository success.

A Word about the IR World

IRs represent an unprecedented opportunity for the transformation of the traditional system of scholarly communication and information dissemination. They have exploded in popularity because of the increasing inability of the traditional system to meet the needs and usage patterns of a user community that is ever larger, more global, and growing more technologically savvy. IRs have been contentious players in the scholarly communication landscape from the start but have achieved a level of participation and use that can no longer be scorned or ignored.

Two main factors account for this. One is the advance in technology, making IRs simple to implement and effective to use, which now allows any institution to implement one with a modest (not to say minimal) commitment of resources. The second is the increase in the acceptance of open access as a creditable and worthy method of disseminating information. The mandate from the National Institutes of Health, which requires deposit of manuscripts resulting from research conducted with funding from the NIH into an open access repository, certainly led the way in this regard, but other efforts, often initiated by scholars and researchers themselves, have occurred in many disciplines. More recently, academic institutions have begun developing internal mandates for open access for their faculty and staff, and as their numbers increase, the place of IRs in the institution, and thus within the larger system of communication, will only increase in importance.

It should come as no surprise that this revolution in the way that scholarly research is communicated is also changing the role of librarians. After all, librarians have had a fundamental position in the traditional system of sharing knowledge for hundreds of years; it is what librarians do. To expect to be able to stand still while that system undergoes profound changes is misguided and, ultimately, self-defeating. While this change can be considered to represent a threat to the profession, if it refuses to acknowledge the change, it also offers an opportunity to reaffirm the centrality of the library in information dissemination and indeed to expand the role of librarians. This is because librarians are well placed to assume a leadership role in the implementation and management of IRs, and indeed this is where oversight is typically centered. This opportunity to play a new role in the scholarly communication system must be seized if librarians are to maintain relevancy in this constantly changing environment. To perform that role, and to perform it well, librarians need to learn the requisite skills, which are not necessarily familiar ones to the profession.

*Open*DOAR, an online list of repositories, includes over 1,000 separate repositories as of this writing. They come in all shapes and sizes, many of them from institutions with fewer resources than most U.S. academic libraries. Critical mass has already been attained, and IRs are not going away. ***Starting, Strengthening, and Managing Institutional Repositories*** will help you join this ever-growing list without exhausting the financial or staff resources of your institution.

Working with IRs is incredibly challenging and rewarding. Especially for librarians, it offers the opportunity to get involved with the scholarly communication system to an extent that has never before been possible. This opportunity, in the face of dwindling financial resources, even before the deepening economic crisis, is one that must be seized. Although the pace of IR development might well be frustrating, it is important to be patient and keep in mind the value of the effort. Nothing less than the transformation of information delivery and the health of our academic libraries and institutions is involved, so get started!

Acknowledgments

I would like to thank Andrea Imre, Electronic Resources Librarian at Southern Illinois University–Carbondale, for her work on the manuscript. Her insight and editorial advice were invaluable, and without them, this book would be much less than what it is.

Introduction

IN THIS CHAPTER:

What Is an Institutional Repository?

Institutional repositories (IRs) are different things to different people. At their most fundamental, they are merely a way to store and provide access to digital information, which any computer or Web site can do. Because of this, they can be used in myriad different ways for different purposes. An academic library, where IRs are most common, will have different purposes for its IR than will a museum, a government agency, or a public library. Even within an institution, such as a research university, different departments will have different uses for the IR. An economics department may want to store and distribute working papers, so fundamental to that community of scholars, while biologists may want to deposit statistical data sets associated with journal articles, and artists may want to distribute video or audio recordings. Some may see the IR as a way to challenge the current system of scholarly communication, with its rewards and high expense, while others are looking for a journal publication platform or a way to distribute unpublished content for which there is no other stable or reliable outlet. The fact is, IRs have the ability to be all things to all people—or nearly so.

For a practical definition of an IR, there is still none better than that offered by Clifford Lynch in 2003:

> A university-based institutional repository is a set of services that a university offers to the members of its community for the management and dissemination of digital materials created by the institution and its community members. It is most essentially an organizational commitment to the stewardship of these digital materials, including long-term preservation where appropriate, as well as organization and access or distribution.

Certainly in the academic setting, IRs have captured the imagination of librarians and promised the solution, or partial solution, to a number of pressing issues: the cost of scholarly communication, the inadequate reach and accessibility of research and creative works of the traditional information delivery system and the new possibilities to ameliorate these inadequacies afforded by the Internet, and the need for preservation of locally created digital content.

Repositories and Scholarly Communication

There can be no doubt that addressing the scholarly communication crisis is one of the fundamental drivers of IR implementation around the world. When the first IR software, Eprints, was planned and created, it was developed as a direct response to this crisis, a way to remove publishers as intermediaries between researchers and their audience. The idea of an IR went hand in hand with the concept of open access, and many of the early adopters or advocates of repositories were also leaders in the spread of open access.

In his seminal manuscript on the subject, Raym Crow (2002: 4) explicitly and prominently spelled out the roles of IRs to:

> Provide a critical component in reforming the system of scholarly communication—a component that expands access to research, reasserts control over scholarship by the academy, increases competition and reduces the monopoly power of journals, and brings economic relief and heightened relevance to the institutions and libraries that support them.

Though many are unwilling to admit it, the scholarly communication system that worked for so many for so long is buckling under inherent weaknesses. This system has existed on a faulty model: scholarly research can be sold for a profit to academic libraries, which have sufficient money to absorb price increases double or triple that of inflation. Academic libraries tried in numerous ways to accommodate these increases without cutting subscriptions, but the collections budget of a university library is a zero sum game: if more money must be spent on journal subscriptions, less money is available for everything else, especially books. Eventually, all the efficiencies were achieved, all the fat was trimmed, until there was no other option but to cut subscriptions. Today, there is almost no academic library in the United States that has not arrived at this point. Consequently, subscriptions are decreasing, and they will continue to do so.

Since Crow's article in 2002, hundreds of new IRs have been established. Their influence on the market of scholarship has been negligible, obviously. Continued increases in the area of 10 percent for journals is a clear indicator of this. Nonetheless, librarians continue to hope that influence is only deferred and that IRs will have a part in the transformation of information dissemination currently underway. For many, they represent one way to make a difference in a system that is busting library budgets, reducing the ability to meet user needs, and forcing the revisioning of research libraries into mere interlibrary loan departments whose functioning rests on the desperate hope that someone, somewhere, had the financial wherewithal to purchase the material being requested.

Expanding Access and Visibility

Regardless of their limited ability to make an impact on the scholarly publishing system, IRs have clearly demonstrated the inadequacy of the system. Millions of downloads are a clear testimony to this and to the need for even more IRs and more content in them. This is a service of indisputable worth, although it may be unclear who is taking advantage of the new availability of previously restricted material. In fact, through the provision of open access to their contents, IRs represent an unprecedented service on the part of their creators and maintainers—usually libraries—to serve a wider audience than they have ever served before.

This is possible because in the traditional system so many are left out—especially less wealthy academic institutions, the general public that has no access to an academic library or comparable resource, and developing countries. This disparity may have been unavoidable in the days of print, but the developments of networking and online publishing in the past 15 years offer the possibility of overcoming this inequality. Repositories were developed to take advantage of these new developments in technology and to distribute information more widely than the prevailing publication system allowed.

Expanded access serves another purpose. It allows for the enhanced visibility of the source institution and its members. Repositories concentrate the output of the institution and present a single site for multiple purposes, including assessment, outreach, and recruitment. Institutional assessment efforts at academic institutions already typically incorporate the collection of details of the publication output of its members; repositories take this to the next level by gathering the content itself. This is a natural growth of a traditional function of the institution. All public universities and many other institutions or their funding sources also require some demonstrable and documented community service component, and repositories can help meet this requirement. Disseminating the results of research openly and freely to the public is already the most common way of meeting this requirement, and repositories do it better than any other mechanism. Finally, the aggregation of all this content supports recruitment efforts by providing an easily accessible record of research interests, accomplishments, and areas of expertise. Repositories make this information available in a way not previously possible to potential students, faculty and other staff, and funders.

Preservation

Preservation is another crucial function of IRs. Libraries have been preserving scholarly and other creative content for almost as long as it has been created. It is incumbent on libraries to pursue this role into the digital future, for the simple reason that no one else is doing it. Already, much content has been lost forever through lack of oversight and foresight. IRs can address this gaping need. This is not to say that they can comprehensively address the complexities of the digital environment, with its rapid rate of change, commercial successes and failures, and vulnerability to economic and social swings. But by gathering and securing content, repositories represent the initial steps necessary for future preservation efforts, and they prepare content for the technical solutions of tomorrow. This is no small task and no small achievement.

New Uses

IRs have evolved over time. In the process of trying to address the issues of the scholarly communication crisis, expand access and enhance visibility, and preserve digital content, repositories have opened possibilities not originally intended or foreseen. While implementers and managers still maintain the lofty goals of spreading scholarly information freely and breaking down the barriers to access, repositories are now used for a wider variety of purposes. These include serving as one part of a marketing plan for an institution, archiving the institution's internal governance documents, managing and distributing theses and dissertations, and more. New uses can be expected to continue to develop and evolve. Successful repositories will be those whose staff are flexible enough to adjust to changing needs, seize unexpected opportunities, and always be open to new possibilities.

Conclusion

IRs have taken the academic world by storm. In less than ten years, their numbers have gone from zero to over 1,000, according to *Open*DOAR, the Directory of Open Access Repositories maintained by Sherpa and housed at Nottingham University in the United Kingdom (www.opendoar.org/index.html). If you calculate a half-time position for each repository—a reasonable estimate and the minimum recommended in Chapter 2—then the equivalent of 500 full-time positions have been created for the management of repositories since their first appearance (and most of these positions are located within a library). Even assuming a conservative figure of $20,000 for the start-up of each one (and other estimates go much higher, as discussed in Chapter 2), then a minimum of $20 million has been invested worldwide in less than a decade. Because costs are ongoing, the true cost is significantly higher. This represents a significant commitment, primarily from universities and their libraries.

Buy-in from information users has been even stronger. No total count exists, but the University of California's repository alone has had over seven million downloads; the number of total downloads from IRs worldwide exceeds well over 15 million. There are those who maintain that institutional repositories have been unsuccessful, but by any measure of their use, this argument falls flat. This should not surprise anyone with an awareness of the trends in the costs of scholarly publishing, particularly librarians; fewer and fewer institutions can afford to meet the demand for information within their institutions. This trend is unlikely to change any time soon.

These two indicators—institutional commitment and strong use—clearly demonstrate that IRs are needed and are not going away. For anyone contemplating the implementation of a new IR, comfort can be found in these two trends and in the community of IR coordinators and developers around the world.

References

Crow, Raym. 2002. "The Case for Institutional Repositories: A SPARC Position Paper." Washington, DC: SPARC. Available: www.arl.org/sparc/bm~doc/ir_final_release_102.pdf (accessed November 11, 2008).

Lynch, Clifford. 2003. "Institutional Repositories: Essential Infrastructure for Scholarship in the Digital Age." ARL Bimonthly Report, No. 226. Available: www.arl.org/newsltr/226/ir.html (accessed November 11, 2008).

Starting and Managing an Institutional Repository: The Steps

I

Librarians and Institutional Repositories: The Perfect Fit

1

IN THIS CHAPTER:

Why Do We Need Institutional Repositories?

Librarians love fads. As soon as a new use of the Internet is announced, some librarian somewhere is seizing the opportunity to co-opt it as part of library service. It is reasonable to ask, before embarking on an effort that will require significant investments of staff time and money as well, is this just another fad? Are we doing it simply because everyone else is? Institutional repositories (IRs) might be viewed in this light by some.

The fundamental—by now almost traditional—justifications for the support of IRs are valid: preserving digital data, enhancing access to and visibility of research, and addressing unsustainable increases in the costs of traditional publication methods (see Introduction). All of these goals are directly related to the mission of libraries. Most of them are altruistic in the sense that they benefit others more than they benefit the library as an organization. In fact, supporting an IR within the library typically means giving up something else—money, staff, and perhaps other library services. Nevertheless, these goals are more properly the domain of the library than any other unit.

Staying Relevant

There is another reason, however, to control the IR from within library walls, less altruistic, perhaps, but just as compelling and potentially advantageous to all. If libraries are to remain relevant, librarians will have to respond to the changing needs of their communities. Shrinking budgets, the availability of online journals and books, the extraordinary success of Internet search engines, and the successful implementation of interlibrary loan programs all combine to reduce the importance and sufficiency of the physical collections within library walls.

In fact, of course, the trend is and has been for some time now increasing demand for the remote use of library resources and services.

DigitalKoans (**http://digital-scholarship.org/digitalkoans**) provides current information on the latest issues and developments in digital scholarly communication, including IRs.

See the Association of Research Libraries' report on academic libraries' new role at **www.arl.org/bm~doc/repository-services-report.pdf.**

For obvious reasons this causes concern in the librarian community, but it can also represent an opportunity to redefine library services. Electronic book collections, virtual reference services, rapid interlibrary loan services—all represent efforts on the part of libraries to address these trends.

Similarly, IRs can be seen as an effort to address trends in the production, dissemination, and use of scholarly materials. By getting involved, librarians demonstrate an awareness of the increasing importance of virtual, informal, and global mechanisms of communication. Indeed, they take a prominent part in the development of such communications. This creates a more involved role for librarians in the cycle of scholarly communication than has typically been possible. By establishing successful repositories, librarians both keep up with the times and increase their role in the research and communication process, thus increasing their visibility, and value, to the community.

Digital Preservation

Libraries also have always been the location for organization and preservation of information inside and outside the academic world. Repositories represent another way to collect and organize digital information, and while by their very nature they can be successful without a rigid structure, their success benefits from the kinds of organization that librarians are trained in: subject organization, metadata (data about data) creation, cross-referencing, etc. It is easier to adjust work assignments of library staff to include IR content description and organization, and much less training is required, than would be the case for other institutional departments.

Furthermore, much of the groundwork—and detailed work—for the development of digital preservation standards is owed to the efforts of librarians, and most libraries are addressing the issue in one form or another. There are, in fact, digital preservation librarians at some institutions, for whom this is their sole job, and many preservation librarian positions are being revised to include digital preservation as a fundamental part of the job. Common sense dictates that digital preservation efforts, such as IRs, reside where the expertise is.

Scholarly Communication Crisis

No doubt the phrase "scholarly communication crisis" will make many librarians wince, as it brings up memories of years of more or less failed attempts to address the growing financial imbalance of the traditional methods of distributing research results and scholarly work. But the fact is, this system is failing, and alternatives are needed to begin to shape the new means of information dissemination of the future. IRs are one part of that answer, and this role is one of the fundamental reasons for their development and for their implementation in institutions around the world. Evidence for this can be found in the large proportion of IRs being housed in academic institutions and, within those institutions, their location inside the library. It is libraries that are hit hardest by the financial burdens associated with the crisis and librarians who have studied it, made it known to the world, and tried to develop answers to it. Their grasp of the problem is essential to the education of all—authors, administrators, readers, etc.—who are in some way involved in perpetuating the problem and who have in their hands the means to address it. Indeed, when working with faculty as potential contributors, raising the issue, in a locally relevant way, is indispensable. This can be done by talking about journal price increases, for example, and the subscription cancellations that have been necessary to account for them.

The Association of Research Libraries maintains one of the best Web sites on scholarly communication at **www.arl.org/sc.**

Who Should Manage an Institution's IR?

Successful implementation of an IR depends on many things, none more important than the decision as to who will coordinate and manage it. There are plenty of repositories with very little content in them. This demonstrates that it is easy enough to build (or have built by a vendor) the repository infrastructure; it is much harder to fill it with content. In other words, the technology is not the stumbling block; low participation from authors and creators is. Emphasizing technical skills as the prerequisite for a repository coordinator is thus misguided; it's the result of a misperception about the nature of building an IR.

Academic librarians have the contacts with faculty and staff that simply do not exist elsewhere on campus. Customarily, each academic department and its faculty members have a librarian assigned to address their library-related questions and needs. This structure and delineation of responsibility is not usually as clearly developed in other university offices, such as information technology departments or offices of research. Only library liaisons (or subject specialists—whatever they are called—they will be referred to as *liaisons* from here on) have it as part of their job descriptions to communicate regularly with all faculty for their assigned departments.

Because of this, effective lines of communication have usually already been developed by liaisons with potential contributors. They are well versed in the varied ways of sharing information, seeking input, and gathering feedback from a disparate set of scholars and researchers, all of which are essential components in the implementation and maintenance of an IR. Liaison responsibilities also include maintaining an awareness of the means of communication among researchers in their assigned departments, so there exists a pool of knowledge in the library about content creation (such as preferred document types), dissemination (such as discipline repositories), and unique needs, even to the level of preferred computer and file formats.

This knowledge represents not only a reduced learning curve for a prospective repository team, it also allows for more effective recruitment from the start, because these liaisons know what material exists that might be ideal for a repository implementation (in beginning, middle, and later stages). In tracking research and publication, combined with regular interaction with researchers, liaisons can identify potential early adopters based on their knowledge of a host of factors regarding the faculty: academic standing (pre-tenure vs. tenured), level of support for new initiatives such as open access publications, and even political leanings or basic personality type. Accurately determining early adopters is important (see Chapter 6), because the early stage of IR development is crucial to building support in the community (and even within the library itself).

IRs should not be static, rigid structures. There need be no restrictive list of approved documents or types of materials that repositories can accept. Indeed, in general, all file formats can be accepted, because in its most basic sense a repository is simply a server—a place to put things and provide access to them. What goes in them is therefore not, or should not be, predetermined. Instead, decisions on content should be based on analysis of researcher communication methods and needs, as well as direct discussions with researchers. In other words, content recruitment should be user driven.

User-driven functions have long defined library services: as a part of regular library functions, circulation records of local holdings are scrutinized; usage reports from electronic databases and journals are regularly downloaded and saved; gate counts are perpetually recorded; new use of technology (such as chat and social networking sites) are monitored and incorporated; focus groups are formed; usability studies are conducted; and feedback is actively solicited and its scarcity a cause of concern.

Resources are regularly adjusted according to the results of all these activities. Especially in vulnerable times—and libraries have been vulnerable to budget cuts for at least three decades now—the natural impulse to adjust to user needs is accelerated by the need to justify money and staff allocations. So, as well as having service as their core missions, flexibility and ability to adapt are essential to libraries' very survival.

This fits well with the purpose and opportunity of IRs. Instead of being decreed from above, individual researchers, and the librarians who work with them, can make the repository do what they need it to do. Instead of adhering to a checklist of permissible uses for the repository, librarians are more likely to push the repository as much as possible to address the needs of the community. Such flexibility is more often than not lacking in other institutional support services, and it increases the value of the IR and its likelihood of success.

How IRs Succeed—or Fail

What constitutes success is subjective and institution specific. For one, 100 documents may meet the threshold, while for another 10,000 may be the target. Perhaps capturing a certain percentage of the output of the institution will define success, or maybe just making accessible a certain set of documents is enough (e.g., theses and dissertations). Despite the difference in definitions of success, the pathways to success—or failure—are the same.

Allocate the Required Resources

Too often, new projects are dumped on staff who already have their hands full. Fad-chasing is a primary cause of this: everyone else is doing this, we need to as well, but we cannot add additional staff, so YOU will have to do it. And by the way, there is no budget for it.

IRs developed in this way are unlikely to succeed. Because success is so dependent on outreach and getting the buy-in of others in the community, success requires enthusiasm, energy, and persistence. Already overworked draftees will not provide any of these.

Every IR needs a leader—one individual recognized as the go-to person and the decision maker. This is not to say that this individual will have absolute authority over everything to do with the IR or be responsible for all aspects of its initiation and maintenance. There are different management arrangements, the selection of which will depend on the institution (see Chapter 2). It simply means that this individual is assigned overall responsibility for the various functions and services of the IR and that his or her work assignment adequately reflects this responsibility.

IRs also take time to develop. Progress can be immediate, but rarely is success. So a long-term commitment has to be made up front and the resources set aside accordingly. No less than three years should be given to assess the success or failure of an IR.

Plan—But Not Too Much

Certain decisions need to be made up front: how will the repository effort be staffed and funded, who will manage it, what platform will be used, what initial policies will be promulgated, and what marketing techniques will be used. Essentially, these are the minimum required to get a repository up and running. Some will want more planning: lengthy and costly surveys to determine contributor needs, details about metadata standards, elaborate assessment plans, etc. While these can be beneficial, limited resources will likely restrict the amount of effort that most institutions can spend on them. Inability to address these issues should not stymie all progress, and overplanning can lead to frustration and gridlock. Furthermore, there is no demonstrable correlation between the resources committed to these ancillary activities and the success (as determined by size or downloads, for example) of an IR. Some of these activities can be undertaken while the IR is in its early stages, if they are determined to be needed. Also, the function and manipulation of IR content will certainly evolve as new technologies are developed, and they cannot be guessed at beforehand. Not all the answers are needed at the point of start-up.

The Skills That Make It Work

Read the literature on IRs, and it is clear that the number one problem is inadequate participation rates—not issues with metadata or how IRs mesh with catalogs or other information systems, etc. This is indicative of the fact that the top priority for any effort should be outreach and content recruitment. The skills for successful outreach and recruitment are the same skills necessary for a successful IR—namely, salesmanship. What is required is the ability to identify potential contributors, modify the recruitment message according to the interests of a given audience or contributor, and convince them of the value and benefit of participation. What will convince one contributor will not work for another—so it is important to have a broad understanding of both the needs of the potential contributor (in relation to the dissemination and preservation of his or her work) and the benefits and uses of IRs. The latter can be selectively emphasized to achieve the highest level of correlation with the former, thereby increasing the likelihood of success. Persistence is then required to follow up as needed.

The Skills That Librarians Have

Librarians have these skills as a result of years of honing them while engaged in similar activities. Marketing other library services to faculty has led to the development and refinement of workable techniques that produce results. Teaching librarians know how to change the delivery of a message in order to achieve the highest level of impact with different types of audiences. Positioning for scarce dollars has made librarians practiced at the art of persuasion.

Beyond this, answering reference questions requires focusing in on an information need. Librarians as faculty or professional researchers share the same communication methods as other faculty and thus have a sense of the limitations and drawbacks of the current system. Certainly they have an awareness of the seriousness of the problems facing all of us in matters of research dissemination and costs and speak about them more knowledgeably than most others.

Finally, there is the issue of copyright (see Chapter 6). IRs have different missions and collect different content, depending on the institution and its members. Most, however, will seek to include some content that has been or is expected to be published in a formal venue, such as a book or journal. This raises the issue of copyright, a thorny one for all concerned. Although some progress has been made in recent years regarding self-archiving and the posting of published content in repositories, it is not always clear-cut what can and cannot be posted. Every document with a publication history or future must be vetted according to the guidelines that are available. These guidelines may exist in different places and require different procedures for ferreting them out, as well as the knowledge to interpret them. With the possible exception of copyright lawyers, no one understands or has had the level of experience with copyright that librarians have had. For this reason alone, it is essential to have librarians with oversight responsibility for the IR. While there have as yet been no major challenges to IR use of published content, there may well be, and it is incumbent on IR staff to adhere to the complicated rules surrounding the use and reuse of this material.

Most IRs are housed in academic institutions, and most of these are run from the library (Primary Research Group, 2007). This is because no unit within the academic institution is as attuned to the need for and benefits of IRs and because librarians have seized the initiative to play a lead role in their development. Often, other units or departments are also involved, and their work can be essential to the success of the repository. Nonetheless, there are more librarians involved in IR development on any given day than are any other departmental staff.

Learning from the Pioneers

Originally, IRs were established with the hopes that researchers, especially faculty, would see the benefits that IRs provide and would rush to have their materials included. There was in essence an "if you build it, they will come" mentality, at least among some early implementers. Predictably, this proved unwarranted, and many were disappointed with the results of their fledgling repositories. Such expectations have been demonstrated to be unrealistic, and no one going into an IR project should harbor them.

Faculty already have a lot on their plates. Participation in an IR is going to compete with many other activities that command their attention. Though the benefits of participation are real and might seem obvious, especially to librarians, this does not automatically translate into action from faculty. The major pitfall early implementers experienced, and which some still fall prey to, is the idea that developing and then marketing this wonderful new service is all that is necessary for a successful and satisfactory result.

In fact, much more is required. There are many components to a successful repository project, which are detailed below, and wishful thinking is not among them.

Conclusion

Throughout this book, just as there is throughout the professional literature on IRs, there will be an emphasis on the need to expand the collections within IRs. Expansion requires leadership, outreach skills, knowledge of methods and trends of communication at the discipline or departmental level, and awareness of copyright issues and of the larger contexts of the political, social, and especially economic aspects of scholarly communication—and all of these map well to the knowledge and skill sets of librarians, more so than any other profession, and thus make them ideal leaders of the IR.

Even so, the decision to take on the start-up and maintenance of an IR cannot be a light one. While it offers unprecedented opportunities to become engaged in the dissemination of information beyond what has been possible in traditional library services, the consequences are clear: staff time and money need to be allocated. How much staff time, and whose, and how much money are the subject of the next chapter.

Keep current on developments in the field via the SPARC-IR listserv (**https://mx2.arl.org/Lists/SPARC-IR**). Another repository listserv is the Repoman listserv (**www.lsoft.com/SCRIPTS/WL.EXE?SL1=REPOMAN-L&H=LISTSERV.INDIANA.EDU**), but it is much less active.

References and Suggested Readings

Markey, Karen, Beth St. Jean, Soo Young Rieh, Elizabeth Yakel, and Jihyun Kim. 2008. "Institutional Repositories: The Experience of Master's and Baccalaureate Institutions." *portal: Libraries and the Academy* 8, no. 2: 157–173.

Primary Research Group. 2007. *The International Survey of Institutional Digital Repositories.* New York: Primary Research Group.

Walters, Tyler O. 2007. "Reinventing the Library—How Repositories Are Causing Librarians to Rethink Their Professional Roles." *portal: Libraries and the Academy* 7, no. 2: 213–225.

Planning, Budgeting, and Staffing

2

While planning can lead to a bureaucratic black hole, where everything is delayed and nothing accomplished, some issues have to be decided on before an institutional repository (IR) is begun—questions that each institution will have to answer. These center around the basic question, do we have the resources necessary to run a successful project? This assessment of resources should be an open and honest one, and planners should be prepared to recommend not going forward if the determination is made that available resources are inadequate to the task. Even at the planning stage, support across the institution can help by pooling resources to make the IR feasible, so seeking this support should be a priority.

IN THIS CHAPTER:

The "Institution" in Institutional

Indeed, an institutional commitment is ultimately necessary if success is to be achieved, because an IR is by its nature an inclusive service, one that requires the involvement of nearly everyone within the institution. In the academic setting, librarians may be the heart of the operation. Liaisons, as mentioned, should spearhead the outreach efforts to their individual departments and constituencies. Technical services staff need to be involved with metadata, preservation standards, and implementation. Depending on the platform, information technology (IT) staff may be heavily involved in keeping the system up and running. Even if that level of support is not required, there is a role for IT staff in ancillary activities, such as streaming content (the most used commercial platforms do not support streaming from their servers). Library administration will need to be involved in first establishing the IR as a priority, including perhaps adjusting the local merit or other reward system accordingly. Administration should also be pushing the IR at university administration levels, representing it as one of the major efforts of the library. An IR is one of the prominent ways for an academic library to demonstrate continued relevance to the institution, meet the immediate needs of its researchers,

and become an active partner in university recruitme
it is an opportunity that often does not get the atten

But the need for support goes beyond the libra
surest way to guarantee uptake by faculty and stud
participation, as happened at Harvard,[1] Stanford,[2] a
be implemented only at the university administrat
reason alone, university administration has a crucial
institutions are prepared to mandate open access for
by the faculty or staff. Even for those institutio
administrations can contribute by vocally and strongly supporting I
development. For implementers, getting statements of support from administration officials can help establish an atmosphere of cooperation that will make IR growth easier. For those using the IR as a database of electronic theses and dissertations, support at the graduate school level is essential, because submission to the IR has to become part of the graduation process; it has to be worked into the list of things to do for all graduate students. Administrators may have their own needs for services that the repository can accommodate; being open to these opportunities and taking them when they present themselves may help to secure administration support.

Importantly, support at the administration level can also translate into funding for the IR. Where this has happened, it has served as an excellent impetus for IR development. It is fundamentally unfair and unwise to have the library (or any other single department) solely responsible for funding the IR. Because it is an institutional effort, it should be institution funded. Two advantages are inherent in this: the funders will have more at stake in the success of the IR, and the IR will be less susceptible to budget cuts and to the impacts of the increasingly burdensome system of scholarly communication they were originally established to overcome.

Planning

The three key elements of a planning body's assessment and proposal are the necessary staffing; the minimal budget; and the recommended platform. All three of these are closely interrelated. Choice of platform will impact the other two elements, and a fundamental element in determining staffing and budgeting requirements is the division between open source and commercial platforms. Commercial platforms require less onsite technical staff but come with a significant subscription fee; open source platforms require not just technical staff but hardware as well, but they do not have subscription fees. Because each institution will have to balance these three elements to determine its own path, the rest of this chapter and the next are devoted to these issues.

Planning the development of an IR must start with an assessment of the necessary commitments in staff and budget. Reports in the literature and professional conferences on IRs give a confused picture and have tended to be skewed by early adopters, who often had access to extraordinary resources that most institutions lack. This is certainly true, for example, for many of the institutions surveyed in the ARL SPEC Kit on Institutional Repositories, which remains the most extensive report on existing and projected IR staff and budgets, as uneven as it is (Bailey, 2006). These reports are difficult to extrapolate from for any given institution and will not be a substitute for careful consideration of the goals of the IR and resources available to achieve those goals.

The assessment of required resources and the ability to provide them has to be done by someone, so the first task is to assign one or more individuals to do this investigation. This body will have responsibility to

- conduct an environmental scan or survey of the experience of institutions who have functioning IRs;
- contact vendors of commercial platforms for demonstrations and price quotes;
- evaluate open source platforms via either implementation or exploration of existing sites;
- prepare a proposal for going forward, including an estimate of costs; and
- establish a timeline for implementation and rollout.

Composition of the planning body will vary. The team that does this preliminary work may not be the one that has ultimate responsibility for starting and managing the IR, should the decision be made to go forward. Because a wide variety of issues will be investigated at this stage, expertise in diverse areas will be useful, especially including technical staff for those considering open source platforms (see Chapter 3), but also including representatives from—or at least consultations with—all of the potentially affected groups. This is necessary in order to attain an accurate picture of the changes in workflow and workload for the institution. Thus, in the library setting, technical services, preservation, liaison, and collection development staff should be involved. Beyond the library, if support is to be sought from other departments or the administration, appropriate representatives should be involved as well.

Another factor determining the size of the group is the sheer amount of work. Environmental scans in particular benefit from the participation of many people, if the pool of those surveyed is to be of adequate size. In other words, there is plenty of work to go around. This may justify a larger planning group.

Typically, at least some of the individuals serving in the planning stages will continue to play a role in IR functions. The success of the planning body, as well as those eventually responsible for IR management, will depend on one or more individuals who are committed to the project and intent on seeing it through, so these individuals should be identified and enlisted from the start. Often, they will be those individuals who have demonstrated the most interest or passion for issues of open access and scholarly communication. Frustration with slow progress or tepid responses should be expected for any IR project, and it is important to have some reserve of energy or commitment to fall back on when results are disappointing.

Budgeting

The question of how much an IR costs and where the funding will come from must be dealt with right from the start. Surveys have solicited information on the cost of an IR, but the numbers are so variable, and the elements funded so vague, that they are mostly uninformative. For example, the ARL survey (Bailey, 2006) reported a mean of $182,550 and a median of $45,000, but these figures are badly skewed by a few big spenders. Jones, Andrew, and MacColl (2006) estimated costs at nearly $90,000 per year (in 2004 dollars). The large number of repositories among smaller institutions, including state universities, indicates that it is quite possible to start and develop an IR with less than this, however. Planning for costs is institution specific, and it is not wise to rely on the reported numbers for any particular institution. It is difficult to come up with a reliable estimate, but, because support is unlikely without a budget, planners need to make an effort to assess the costs before moving forward with an implementation. The following discussion outlines the major components of the budget for an IR.

Assessing the cost of an IR primarily has to take into account two main components: the equipment (hardware and software) and the personnel. Marketing and training costs also need to be accounted for. The costs associated with each of these components will depend on which software is used. In general, costs can be estimated based on whether an open source or a commercial product is used.

Hardware/Software

Open source software is, of course, free. The hardware, at a minimum, will include the server needed to deliver the content. The cost of a server depends on a number of factors. Ordinarily, existing server configuration within the institution will at least partially determine what type of server is purchased. The size of the server also impacts cost, and a balance has to be struck between anticipated storage need and available funding. Here again, institutional goals need to be considered when planning. Video files, for example, consume an enormous amount of memory, especially in preservation formats; an institution planning on storing a high number of videos will need more storage than one focusing on articles and technical reports.

Realistically, a single server is inadequate to provide a reliable repository service, because backup is necessary in case something happens to the live server. A backup server is typically not of the same quality as the live server, because it is meant solely to provide access during an emergency and to ensure that content is not lost. Nevertheless, costs are in the thousands. Additionally, with software such as DSpace, a test server is needed, or at least highly recommended, to test new updates before going live with them to ensure proper implementation and functioning. Again, while this server can be less expensive than the live server, costs are still in the thousands. Consultation with IT staff will be necessary for anyone going this route.

The other option is to subscribe to an IR service from a commercial provider. Unfortunately, for the most commonly subscribed commercial service, bepress' Digital Commons, pricing is considered confidential. The same is true for those integrated library systems vendors that have created an IR module, the most well-known one being Ex Libris' DigiTool. For these products, quotes have to be requested. BioMed Central makes pricing for its product, Open Repository, openly available on its Web site (www.openrepository.com/products).

Personnel

Hardware and software are only one component of an IR budget. Indeed, the largest cost associated with an open source repository is staffing. Because there is no contracted help available, this service has to be provided in-house. While some functions can be fulfilled by an IT staff member with knowledge of server maintenance, others will require the skills of a programmer with knowledge of Java and/or other languages. This ability is required for all updates, not to mention locally designed adaptations to the core software. For the Fedora platform, this level of support is significantly higher (see Chapter 3).

No consensus exists on the required amount of staffing for an open source platform. However, some generalities have been revealed in the course of many IR development hours: a designated technical staff person is essential. Because the IR is a high-profile service with at least the potential for significant contact with faculty or other important stakeholders, the IR must be established as a high priority for that staff member. Especially during start-up, it is self-defeating to advocate for adoption of the service and then be unable to meet the requests of the contributor pool. Often, contributors' needs are not matched exactly with out-of-the-box configuration (true for any platform). Having to tell a contributor who has been solicited for input that his or her needs can only be addressed at some time in the future, when the technical staff can get around to it, will discourage participation and threaten the success of the IR. It may be that at certain times demand on the technical staff's time will be minimal or even none; but it is necessary to have them prepared to be able to offer quick turnaround service when required.

In addition to technical support, outreach efforts demand personnel time as well. Indeed, given the well-documented difficulties in populating IRs, aggressive, persistent outreach efforts consume—or should consume—the lion's share of the personnel commitment. Again, no consensus exists, and an adequate staffing assignment will to some extent be determined by the goals of the institution. Because content recruitment has been such an issue, it is safe to say that the more staffing devoted to it, the better the repository will be. Especially in the early stages of development, it is necessary for IR staff to actually do some of the manual work of submission, and there again, the more hours on the job, the more content there will be.

Indeed, repository size clearly correlates with staff size. Most institutions have found a half-time coordinator to be the absolute minimum for sustained development. Planning for a modest pace of development requires at least that, so budgeting for staff should be based on the costs—salary and benefits—at that level. For a commercial product implementation, this may be completely sufficient for an institution's need. For an open source repository, many institutions employ both a technical staff member and an outreach coordinator. The technical staff member's commitment is flexible, as mentioned, but a safe number for planning purposes would also be 50 percent.

Clearly, an open source repository is going to have more staff costs than a commercial one. In addition, there are the server costs. Whether these combined costs exceed those of a commercial implementation will depend on the local staffing costs, what level of staff is hired and for how many hours, and quality and quantity of hardware purchased versus the cost of the commercial service.

Training and Marketing

Whether an open source or a commercial platform is used, the staff needs to be trained, and the service needs to be marketed. These too require funding. Numerous and increasing conferences and workshops address IR implementation and development, and, especially in the early stages, IR staff should expect to attend these to the extent possible. Open Repositories (www.openrepositories.org), an international conference, is an important venue, especially for open source repositories, as it includes user groups for Fedora, Eprints, and DSpace. Other events occur with some regularity at Association of Research Libraries, Association of College and Research Libraries, and American Library Association events.

Marketing costs must be accounted for and should be expected to be high in the beginning and then decrease as time goes on. Distributable materials such as handouts and brochures will need to be produced, and, as forums and other meetings with local or prominent speakers may help spread the word, they may be warranted as well. All of this costs money. Estimates should include attendance of one or two meetings per year and production and distribution of an attractive brochure to, at a minimum, all of the faculty or researchers for the institution. It is not unrealistic to estimate $5,000 to $10,000 for these support activities for the first year and something less than that for at least the subsequent three to five years. It is of course possible to get by on less than this, but every opportunity should be taken to make the case that running an IR on the cheap is a losing strategy.

Funding Sources

Theoretically, funding should come from the institution. In practice, thus far, it almost always comes from the library (Bailey, 2006; Rieh et al., 2007). This represents a reallocation from other services or functions in most cases, not new funding. Realistically, this should be expected for new IR implementations.

Some have had success acquiring financial support from the institution for their IR. Most often this comes from an office of research, the provost, or similar sources. Some success has been reported in gaining administration support by selling the IR as a way to help in research assessment activities (Simpson and Hey, 2006). If an IT department is involved, it may also contribute funding (as well as personnel); sharing the cost of the IR may be one reason to involve the IT department, even to the point of determining the platform chosen. Although already competitively sought after, student fees, such as technology fees, may also be won, for example, for an electronic theses and dissertations service within the IR. More rarely, individual schools or departments may help cover costs if the faculty members (or the administrators) see a compelling need to have the service.

Finally, some have successfully received grants to support the IR or some component of it. Success may be more often achieved here if a specific collection or aspect of the IR is used as the basis of the grant proposal. It may also be more likely to procure grant funding if proposals are made from a consortium or other group—which also provides additional benefits.

The main source for grants is the Institute of Library and Museum Services (**www.imls.gov**). Because IRs cover so much content, fund seekers can be creative in applying for grants. For example, the National Endowment for Humanities awards Preservation and Access Research and Development grants, which could be used to develop new content for the IR. The site **www.grants.gov** is a good place to get started in the search for grant funding.

Consortia

Consortium support of an IR can mean reduced expenditures for staffing and equipment for each individual institution. In particular, costs for server and storage and technical support can be shared (Estlund and Neatrour, 2007). Centralized funding, such as exists for the SUNY Digital Repository, can help distribute the costs so that smaller institutions, which might be unlikely to implement an IR on their own, have the necessary infrastructure in place to build their own presence. Also, maximizing expertise, particularly where consortial sharing allows the hiring of new staff, may lead to more sophisticated services than individual institutions can achieve. There is a trade-off of course; participating institutions will have to abide by any policies and constraints determined by the consortium or other administering body. Given the idiosyncrasies of scholars and their research, and their resistance to pigeon holing, this may cause some friction and even some failure at a particular site. Nevertheless, for those unable to initiate and maintain such an undertaking on their own, this kind of shared responsibility and funding may be hard to resist. Given a difficult economic climate, and the need to do more with less, consortial IRs may become even more attractive.

See the SUNY Digital Repository at **http://dspace.sunyconnect.suny.edu**.

Staffing

It is important to recognize that determining staffing is not just a matter of calculating salaries and benefits and throwing them into the scale of costs. Regardless of platform chosen, successful IR management and development requires certain definable skills and characteristics. Any recommendation on IR staffing must take these qualities into account. In addition, because IRs are most successful if they involve the participation of a variety of staff, some leadership structure must be determined, and a leader (or leaders) must be designated to coordinate the work of everyone.

Some designated IR staffing, either from reassignment or creation of a new position, is essential for a successful IR program. But staffing must be the right staffing in order to achieve success. This means that the skill sets of the staff must match the needs of the IR project. As we have seen, the skill sets of librarians match up well with the general needs for an IR; but not all librarians will have the skills necessary for IR work. A detailed examination of the requisite skills will help to identify the best fit for any given institution.

Furthermore, a clear identification of goals for the IR should help in determining the desired skills and aptitudes necessary to achieve them for a particular institution. Different institutions will have different goals and purposes for an IR, and staffing needs will vary accordingly. Nevertheless, while contributor pools, content types, and audience will all vary, still the primary goal for the early stages should be the same across all institution types: namely, promoting and demonstrating the IR's effectiveness and benefits to the institution and, particularly, to the contributor pool. This means outreach.

Skill Set Required for Implementing and Developing an IR

- Boldness
- Knowledge
- Persuasiveness
- Persistence
- Flexibility

In this sense, IR implementation and development is like nothing so much as salesmanship, and it requires the same set of skills: boldness, knowledge, persuasiveness, persistence, and flexibility. Each of these qualities merits further discussion.

- **Boldness.** Because the IR will only rarely sell itself, it is necessary to make the initial contact with members of the contributor pool, including knocking on doors and making "cold calls." Some failures in recruitment efforts should be expected in the form of outright refusals to participate; this will not deter the effective IR staff. Shyness, low self-esteem, or social awkwardness and IRs do not mix. What is needed is someone who is confident in his or her own abilities and the project and who is led by the courage of his or her convictions. This will go a long way to achieve production and success over an extended period of time.
- **Knowledge.** This includes knowledge of the potential users: how do they communicate with colleagues and others? What is the nature of the research output—not just the final form, such as book or journal articles or live performance, but the accompanying information as well? It also includes knowledge of developments in scholarly communication in order to talk intelligently about the need for IRs, open access, the economics of publishing, and the uses and benefits of technology in research communication. Potential contributors will raise surprisingly various questions, and a good grasp of the issues will go a long way to answering those questions and making the contributors feel comfortable not just with the IR, but with its staff as well. This is essential.

- **Persuasiveness.** Essentially, this is the ability to take the knowledge described above and develop it into a targeted message for a particular potential contributor. IRs have many benefits; they will vary in the strength of their appeal to different contributors, and, given the limited time and attention most contributors will be able or willing to spare for a sales pitch, it will be important to know what benefits to highlight.
- **Persistence.** For many potential contributors, nothing will put an IR at the top of their to-do list. There are simply too many other things vying for their attention. Therefore, repeated contact, nudging, and coaxing will always be part of the process of gathering content. A failure to follow through on the part of a contributor is not a reflection on the IR or its marketers, and revisiting the contributor is not an imposition; it is an imperative. It simply comes with the territory.
- **Flexibility.** Some contributors will be tech savvy, and others won't. Some will have enough time to do submissions themselves, and some will barely be willing to send a CV. Establishing a firm set of rules about how contributions will be done and sticking to those rules is a losing strategy. It may be necessary for IR staff to do some of the actual submissions themselves, including verifying the legality of making the submission, finding the full text, and entering metadata. If this is viewed as beneath the qualifications—or dignity—of the IR staff member, then he or she is the wrong staff person. At some point the IR may become so established that members of the institution may be obliged to participate, or participation may even be mandated; until then, flexibility will be necessary to develop the fragile new service.

All of these qualities, theoretically at least, map nicely to the skills expected for and developed by liaisons, or subject specialists, in the academic library setting. Therefore, their participation, if not leadership, is essential for success. On the other hand, without staff who have these skills, an IR is unlikely to succeed. Perhaps the only exception would be for an institution that has mandated repository participation.

In fact, in combination with a commercial IR platform, requiring little or no technical skills, the qualities described form a necessary and sufficient combination for a successful IR coordinator. It is possible with a commercial platform, as has been demonstrated by a number of institutions, to not only get by on but to achieve some measure of success with nothing more than one person who possesses some or all of these qualities. This cannot be said for institutions using an open source platform. The implications for this on budgeting were discussed earlier.

This is not to say that other skills are not valuable for a successful IR effort, on any platform. Maximizing the value and appeal of a repository will require the repository to possess a number of other attributes, including the appropriate hierarchical structure, accurate and appropriate metadata, analyzing and distributing download data, new content notification, etc. Each of these requires different skills, including knowledge of design and usability, metadata standards and interoperability, basic data manipulation, and, potentially, programming. In addition, maximizing the outreach and support effort requires oversight, so able leadership and planning skills are valuable as well.

Obviously, for a locally implemented open source solution such as DSpace, technical skills are going to be essential as well. Such IR instances require considerable programming skills in order to get the repository up and running, to maintain it, to install and implement updates, and to add locally created modifications. The type of programming skills are platform dependent and are discussed more in the next chapter.

Identifying the appropriate staff and bringing them together is one thing; coordinating their work is another. Coordination is important in order to deliver a consistent message, follow through on priorities established to achieve the most impact, ensure development across a diverse pool of contributors, monitor progress and highlight success, etc. This requires some level of leadership.

Leadership

Leadership may be of two types, each of which may evolve over time. The first type of leadership can be defined in a coordinator's role, one who has responsibility for oversight of the entire IR operation: planning, implementing, maintaining, and extending the IR. The coordinator may have to oversee the work of many efforts, including technical, outreach, and planning. As such, much of this leadership is behind the scenes. Organization and management skills are needed for this role.

The second type of leadership is more exclusively out front: serving as the primary contact for the IR to the institution and beyond and heading the publicity effort, including meeting with potential contributors and supporters. Speaking, presentation, and marketing skills are required in this role.

These two roles may or may not be vested in one person. As the first requires management skills above all and the second public relations skills, it may be difficult to find one person who can excel in both. Because each is essential for a successful IR, separating the roles and designating one individual for each may be the best strategy. Leadership roles may change over time as well, as start-up requires considerable effort in coordination, and certain aspects of development will need decreasing attention thereafter: project planning and development of policies are the big ones, but creation of marketing materials, interface design decisions, and site administration training also fall into this category.

It cannot be overemphasized that the primary needs for all leadership roles are a strong belief in the project and the sincere desire to see it succeed. Because it is so often the case that the IR is an add-on to staff responsibilities, it runs the risk of being overlooked or deemphasized by overworked individuals. Only the committed should be entrusted with the role of seeing it through; if there is no one committed, and no ability to hire someone who is, the decision to pursue an IR should be reviewed and, probably, revoked.

Teaming

Another way to fulfill the leadership functions is via a team, which is especially attractive for institutions that simply are unable to designate IR work as a significant component of any specific staff member's work assignment. This assumes, of course, that there are enough people working on the IR to warrant a team. Indeed, for a majority of institutions, this is exactly the working structure for IR support. While allowing for a more or less equitable distribution of work, and capitalizing on the different abilities of the participants, this strategy often suffers from an inadequate commitment to the IR effort. It simply becomes one more thing for an already overburdened staff to do. Roles may change here as well, and it is not unusual for an initial implementation team to give way to a maintenance team once the framework is in place. The leadership team is not merely everyone working on the IR; in fact, for most institutions, it should be a small subset.

For all the reasons laid out in this chapter and in Chapter 1, some representation from liaisons is essential for the team. Other factors that determine who else is included will depend on the institution, the platform in use, and the collections being targeted. Certainly library technical services representation is always warranted, as metadata, even if not emphasized for a given IR, is a fundamental component of the collections. Someone with knowledge of digital preservation standards and requirements may also be desirable. For open source platforms, technical staff is essential, as they will be responsible for not only maintaining the hardware and software but also determining what functions and enhancements are or are not possible and the demand on staff time they will require. This will be crucial in setting priorities. More difficult to achieve, but no less important for that, is the inclusion of someone from the faculty, researchers, or other contributor pool who can provide insight into the needs of those they represent. Even if the pool is so diverse that no one can be expected to competently represent all the constituents, a representative will have valuable contributions to make to the administrative team.

Conclusion

Planning an IR begins with identifying the personnel responsible not just for its implementation but also for its ongoing management as well, choosing the platform that best fits the goals, needs, and resources of the institution and estimating the costs associated with the project. The costs include personnel, hardware and software, and marketing and other development activities. Determination of the appropriate staff and estimation of costs will depend on the platform chosen, and this is the subject of the next chapter.

Notes

1. Passed February 2008 by the Faculty of Arts and Sciences. This was subsequently also adopted by the Law School. See http://osc.hul.harvard.edu/OpenAccess/policytexts.php.
2. Passed June 10, 2008, by the School of Education. See http://ed.stanford.edu/suse/faculty/dspace.html.
3. Passed March 18, 2009, by the Faculty. See http://info-libraries.mit.edu/scholarly/faculty-and-researchers/mit-faculty-open-access-policy.

References

Bailey, Charles. 2006. *Institutional Repositories (SPEC Kit 292)*. Washington, DC: Association of Research Libraries.

Estlund, Karen and Anna Neatrour. 2007. "Utah Digital Repository Initiative: Building a Support System for Institutional Repositories." *D-Lib Magazine* 13, no. 11/12: 1–1.

Jones, Richard, Theo Andrew, and John MacColl. 2006. *The Institutional Repository*. Oxford: Chandos.

Rieh, Soo Young, Karen Markey, Beth St. Jean, Elizabeth Yakel, and Jihyun Kim. 2007. "Census of Institutional Repositories in the U.S.: A Comparison across Institutions at Different Stages of IR Development." *D-Lib Magazine* 13, no. 11/12: 1–1.

Simpson, Pauline and Jessie Hey. 2006. "Repositories for Research: Southampton's Evolving Role in the Knowledge Cycle." *Program: Electronic Library & Information Systems* 40, no. 3: 224–231.

Institutional Repository Platforms

3

IN THIS CHAPTER:

- ✔ Criteria for Evaluating Platforms
- ✔ Open Source Platforms
- ✔ Commercial Platforms
- ✔ Final Thoughts
- ✔ References and Suggested Readings

Criteria for Evaluating Platforms

What are the issues to consider when exploring institutional repository (IR) platforms? The answer to this question will depend on the goals for the repository. A repository can be as simple or as complex a service as is desired; simpler goals, such as a way to distribute and preserve content, require fewer and simpler questions to analyze. A more sophisticated service will require deeper analysis of platforms, potentially including their ability to operate with other services and systems (most commonly integrated library systems), support of multiple metadata schemes, journal publishing, batch uploading, etc. Each institution will have to decide what factors should be included and emphasized in their analysis.

Practically speaking, however, for most institutions that are risk averse and are trying to do the best they can on limited supplies of money and personnel, one consideration has to be the standing or popularity of the platform in the library and repository community. For one reason, this guarantees some level of support from other implementers and the opportunity to benefit from the experience of those who have gone before. While there are a number of repository platforms, only a few can meet this benchmark: on the open source side, DSpace, Eprints, and (for those with adequate resources) Fedora; for commercial providers, Digital Commons, Open Repository, CONTENTdm®, and DigiTool. This chapter considers these platforms.

One of the key questions that determine platform selection will be the availability of *staffing*. As discussed in Chapter 2, with a commercial platform, it is possible to get by with one 50 percent full-time employee (FTE) position, with this staff member focusing on outreach efforts and content recruitment. With an open source platform, this position is still necessary, and at a minimum a 50 percent FTE position for technical support should also be planned. If this technical position is not available for specific assignment to the IR, selecting an open source platform is a mistake. In addition, specific technical skills are necessary to operate an open source platform. Some will involve server maintenance, but the more tricky part is any programming requirements—and all of the open source platforms require some programming knowledge, at a minimum for installation. Specific codes for these platforms are indicated later. Again, if there is no local expertise with that particular code available, choosing that open source platform would be a mistake.

The *structure* of the repository also needs consideration. Each platform handles the hierarchical structure a little differently, and it is important to examine the platforms to ensure that there is a match between the needs of a particular institution and what is provided. The different structures are described later, but there is no substitute for actually visiting some Web sites for any given platform and scouting around to see how things look.

Structure is closely tied to *administration*, because it is usually possible to designate different administrators for different sections and layers of the repository. This is an important feature if sharing the work and/or implementing a decentralized model of management is a goal. Administration involves not just the ability to designate a number of administrators, but also determining what rights those administrators will have. Open source platforms will generally allow more flexibility for administrators to create the look and feel they desire, while commercial platforms may not allow much modification or customization. The amount of flexibility offered by a commercial provider may be hard to determine beforehand, but an environmental scan, including direct discussions with subscribers, may help to answer specific questions. Pilot projects, with no ongoing commitment from the institution, can also aid in this determination, but not all commercial providers will offer one.

Metadata's importance in determining platform selection—or indeed any aspect of repository development and maintenance—is open to dispute. The answer you get may depend on whether you are talking to a cataloger or a liaison, a faculty member or a programmer. Metadata (beyond the basic author and title information, which all platforms support) may be either superfluous or essential, depending on the goals for the repository. If discoverability is the only essential, it can well be argued that full-text searching of documents trumps any metadata description. On the other hand, long-term preservation efforts of digital content, including repository content, which have been underway for some time, are dependent on extensive (and time-consuming) metadata (Wheatley, 2004). One essential is that the metadata be harvestable via the OAI-PMH protocol, and all of the platforms discussed later meet this requirement. Metadata and OAI-PMH are examined more fully in Chapter 7.

Metadata also plays a role in the system's *interoperability*, another aspect to consider. All platforms support searching via Google, so this is not a concern. If it is seen to be desirable to have the IR searchable together with the catalog, however, or other local systems, planners will need to investigate the technical issues accordingly.

Planners should take a good look at the *support* sites offered by platform providers, for all stages of development, to determine the suitability and sufficiency of what can be found there. This is particularly true of open source sites that have no designated support staff available, and Web sites, wikis, and discussion lists may be the only option to find a solution to a problem. The amount, organization, and quality of the information provided on these support sites vary, and their adequacy must be taken into consideration.

The decision on platform selection should carefully weigh *long-term* issues, not merely what is best for the immediate future. An IR is a long-term—perpetual, essentially and ideally—commitment, and this endurance is at one time the *purpose* and the *appeal* of the service. To promise stability and endurance to the community only to change platforms, and possibly URLs, structure, or method of access, is self-defeating. Nevertheless, there have been instances, and will no doubt continue to be more, where institutions have switched platforms. There can be many reasons for this—changes in personnel, new initiatives at a higher level (such as the state), failed commercial ventures, etc. To protect the IR against these changes, it is necessary to ensure that the content and the metadata that are loaded are movable, capable of migration to another platform.

One more element of the analysis warrants discussion. This is the distinction between open source and commercial platforms. Although some of the practical implications of choosing one or the other have already been touched upon, for some this decision may be a philosophical issue as well. Sometimes, an institution or an administrator may be determined to implement open source solutions whenever and wherever possible. Others may deem open source software to be unreliable or, at any rate, too demanding for their particular situation and require a commercial service. Choosing between these distinct options is likely to be the first decision implementers will have to make, and the platforms described later are separated accordingly.

An interesting way to see the global implementation of IRs is via Repository 66 (**http://maps.repository66.org**), a mashup that shows implementation by platform on a map of the world.

One last note: For both open source and commercial platforms, change is inherent and can be frequent. Support sites and vendor contacts should be utilized at the time of decision making in order to learn about the latest developments and current states of services, software, and support.

Open Source Platforms

Open source means more than just *free*. At its simplest, open source means that no payment is required for the product, and its source code is readily available and can be modified (Gibbons, 2004). More significantly, open source represents a commitment to a way of developing services and delivering content unfettered by the need to earn profits and please shareholders. It is a distinct change from the traditional system of product development, and it is heavily dependent on the participation, not just consumption, by its user communities. This does not mean that every implementing institution is required to contribute hours of coding or testing, but it does mean that the product is only as good as the sum of the efforts of its implementers.

More on the definition and philosophy behind open source code can be found at the Open Source Initiative's Web site at **http://opensource.org**.

Open source platforms may be said to more closely match the goals of IRs than do commercial products. Open source platforms for open access content offer a consistent and attractive philosophical principle. IRs are at least partly designed to compete with the traditional commercial systems of publishing and information dissemination (Crow, 2002), and only using an open source platform can accomplish this goal while truly freeing researchers and their content. Open source platforms may have technical restrictions, but they allow for local customization and re-purposing that is simply not always possible with commercial providers. The latter are in the hands of companies that have more or less fixed ideas about how they envision their product working, what it can do, what developments they will pursue, and what exceptions they will permit to their customers.

The freedom that open source platforms bring comes with a price, however. Customization requires long-term maintenance, and some platforms may require the customization to be done each time a new update to the code is loaded. Regardless, local technical support must be devoted to the repository; the system must be learned and learned well for local modifications; and servers must be acquired, maintained, and backed up. Each institution must evaluate honestly and openly these commitments against its available staff and resources.

DSpace

For more information on DSpace, visit **www.dspace.org**.

According to *Open*DOAR (www.opendoar.org), DSpace is far and above the most common repository platform implemented worldwide, with over 350 instances (an implementation of any platform at an institution is called an *instance*). DSpace holds the preeminent position in repository platforms in the United States and also has a sizable market share around the world. It was developed between 2000 and 2002 by a well-funded collaborative effort between the Massachusetts Institute of Technology (MIT) and Hewlett-Packard.

Not only did this effort result in DSpace, it also laid the groundwork for many of the other aspects of repository development and implementation that have come to be adopted by repository staff everywhere. For example, many repositories provide information on the different types of file formats they support and the level of commitment they make toward preserving them. For most sites, this language and list of file types is taken verbatim from the original, produced at MIT (see http://libraries.mit.edu/dspace-mit/build/policies/index.html).

The collaboration between MIT and Hewlett-Packard led to a remarkable product that has proven successful at hundreds of institutions. Since the rollout of DSpace, first Hewlett-Packard and then MIT moved away from formal support of the software. Since 2007, the DSpace Foundation has taken over the leadership role for the continued development and support of DSpace and its community of users.

Installation and Base Technology

DSpace is freely available at http://sourceforge.net/projects/DSpace. It requires a server that stores the files that are loaded (the server is typically run on UNIX); a Postgres or Oracle database that creates the structure and allows the management of data within the repository; a Web application server (using Apache Tomcat or Jetty) that delivers the Web pages; and the user interface, which is how the world interacts with the repository and which is currently available in either the Java Server Page interface or the Manakin interface. The code itself is written in Java.

Structure and Administration

Perhaps because DSpace was developed at an academic institution, the structure it uses matches well with the structure of a typical academic institution. A repository is divided into communities, which can be further subdivided into as many subcommunities as desired. Each community or subcommunity then contains collections, which house the actual documents or other items.

Administration is accomplished by assigning privileges to "e-people" and "groups." An e-person is essentially an e-mail address with some additional information attached to it (name, password, and alerting information); groups are just aggregations of e-people. Privileges can then be assigned to both e-people and groups. An e-person assigned to the group then has his or her own assigned privileges, as well as any that are assigned to the group.

Metadata

DSpace supports descriptive, administrative, and structural metadata. It uses qualified Dublin Core and requires only a title, language, and date of submission (Smith et al., 2003). DSpace provides the ability to configure multiple schemas beyond Dublin Core and select metadata fields from a mix of configured schemas. It also supports OAI-PMH, enabling harvesting of repository content by any service providers that use this protocol (see Chapter 7 for more on OAI-PMH).

Special Features

DSpace incorporates the use of the CNRI Handle System® for establishing persistent identifiers to ensure that the URLs for the contents will endure. There is full support for the management of electronic journals. Checksum, a procedure to test for the integrity of stored data, is an automated feature.

The use statistics package that comes with DSpace has long been viewed as inadequate. For one thing, getting numbers of downloads is not possible; only item views are reported (as of this date). An item is viewed when the title page is opened. This is not compliant with the standards for the reporting of electronic journal use so widespread in the library profession and does not give a clear indication of actual use. This makes assessment more subjective. Information includes views of collections and communities, OAI requests, searches, and user logins. Statistics are available in monthly and total reports.

Support

As mentioned, DSpace is the most common platform in use. This translates into the largest support group as well. Open source software usually brings with it a body of users who are helpful and supportive, and DSpace is no exception. Its support group, the DSpace Forum (www.dspace.org/index.php/Forum), has over 4,000 users. There are instances all over the world, which makes DSpace a good choice anywhere, because there is a good chance there will be fellow users somewhere nearby. There is also a well-developed wiki (http://wiki.DSpace.org/index.php/DSpace Resources) with an immense amount of information, including documentation and guidelines on installation, customization, and development. There are even chat rooms dedicated to DSpace. However, while all this is undeniably valuable, it must be understood that there is no one to call on the telephone to ask for help for a specific problem. There is no dedicated support staff to fall back on, and, while it would be inaccurate to say that with DSpace you are on your own, without the technical staff onsite to deal with issues related to UNIX or Java or Tomcat or Postgres, or all of these, it may be a struggle to maintain a stable and reliable service.

Price

An institution should expect to spend a minimum of $40,000 on a new implementation, according to DSpace administrators (see www.DSpace.org/index.php/Hardware/25-Hardware-Requirements-Server-Size-Disk-Space.html).

BOTTOM LINE

Pros

DSpace has the largest support group in the world and the best online support available. The large user base means many people are working on new features and add-ons. There is a high degree of customization allowed.

Cons

Significant technical skills are required. Use statistics are inadequate.

Eprints

For more information on Eprints, visit **www.eprints.org**.

Eprints holds second place among repository platforms, and it is the most common choice in Europe. Its use in the United States and, indeed, worldwide is much more restricted, however. Eprints was and is developed at the School of Electronics and Computer Science at the University of Southampton in the United Kingdom, and it was first released in 2000. In a sense, it is a misnomer to label Eprints an open source platform, because the developers do not allow access and modifications to the code, a hallmark of open source software. It is, however, possible to contribute plug-ins and scripts. For a price, it is possible to join the "Eprints Community," an official body that is given privileged access to Eprints developers and to have some involvement in Eprints governance and developments.

Installation and Base Technology

Eprints can be downloaded free at http://files.eprints.org/view/type/release.html. Eprints was built to run on UNIX machines and now can be run on Mac OS-X and Windows Vista and XP computers. It requires Apache as the Web server and uses MySQL for the database. Eprints is written in Perl.

Structure and Administration

Eprints organizes content by subject or group. Groups have an unlimited number of subgroups. There are not collections or series for groups, but items can be assigned an item type category (such as article, conference paper, etc.) and the system allows groups to be sorted by these categories. Prior to version 3.1, released late in 2008, there was no Web interface for the modification of this structure; each addition, deletion, or edit required the use of a script. The new Web interface for basic administration functions may make Eprints a more attractive option. Administration privileges are granted to users or groups of users.

Metadata

Eprints allows administrative, descriptive, and structural metadata. It is OAI-PMH compliant. Metadata fields are assigned to types, which determine how that field can be used and displayed. It is possible to export data in Dublin Core, METS, and MODS simply by choosing from a drop-down list. Exporting metadata to RSS, XML, and bibliographic management programs such as EndNote is also supported. There is support for importing metadata from other services.

Special Features

Eprints now supports an author name authority via either metadata fields previously used or an authority created by an administrator. This allows for autocompletion of author fields and avoids data entry errors, providing consistency and authority across the repository. Eprints adds thumbnails and previews of all files. Eprints does assign permanent URLs. The CNRI Handle System® is not supported, but it is possible to map to handles.

Gathering usage data for Eprints repositories is not easy or straightforward. A new tool was introduced in 2007, IRStats (Interoperable Repository Statistics), but it still has kinks. IRStats provides data by author or subject and also includes the ability to show the data in different types of graphs. It requires Perl, AWStats, Postgres, or MySQL and a Web server. Information about installation and configuration can be found at http://trac.eprints.org/projects/irstats. An older tool was developed at the University of Tasmania in 2006 and is still available at http://eprints.utas.edu.au/262.

Support

Eprints offers a lower level of support for its general users than does DSpace. It has a technical discussion list, which is unsearchable, and a wiki (see http://wiki.eprints.org/w/Main_Page).

However, there is another option for those who would like an open source solution but feel the need for more support: *Eprints Services.*

This is a subscription service offered by the Eprints developers. Four packages are offered, with differential pricing based on the level of service:

- Value package
  - Basic training for the repository manager to set up and run the repository
  - Basic-level service agreement, which covers e-mail help in the initial operating period
  - Specified turnaround on issues/fixes
  - Bulletin board support
- Professional package
  - Builds the repository, tailoring it to the institution's needs
  - Provides support to administrator
  - Provides advice on institutional policies
  - Provides advice on best practices
  - Specified turnaround time on problems
  - Ongoing e-mail support
- Premium package (professional package included)
  - Fully hosted service
  - Initial feasibility and impact assessment
  - Support for researchers depositing their work
  - Training for the administrator in all areas of repository support and development, including advocacy
  - Priority turnaround on issues/fixes
  - Telephone helpline
- Hosting service
  - Includes upgrades, fixes, and backup

With any or all of these packages, the institution then has a dedicated staff member they can contact with problems, just as is possible with other commercial providers. More information is available at www.eprints.org/services/sales. Pricing is based on the package chosen and increases significantly from the value to the premium packages. Eprints Services has to be contacted for exact pricing (see www.eprints.org/services). Finally, training courses are offered periodically, usually at the University of Southampton, but occasionally elsewhere. The training course lasts two days and focuses on the technical aspects of Eprints repository management.

BOTTOM LINE

Pros

Eprints is easy to install. Various support packages make it an option for a variety of institutions.

Cons

Making changes to the repository, including adding new groups, is involved. Use statistics modules are difficult to implement. It is not, by strict definition, an open source platform.

Fedora

What is Fedora, besides a hat? It's an acronym, which stands for Flexible Extensible Digital Object and Repository Architecture. It is not an IR per se but an architecture on which many digital services can be built, including an IR. Among many others, an important implication of this is that the interface for an IR has to be locally built, as there is none that comes standard with the software.

For more information on Fedora, visit **www.fedora-commons.org**.

Fedora was developed by the University of Virginia and Cornell University. It was first released to the public in 2003. Because of a dispute with Red Hat, which wanted to use the name Fedora for its Linux operating system, the Fedora under consideration here has become known as the Fedora Repository.

Installation and Base Technology

Fedora is available at SourceForge (http://sourceforge.net/project/platformdownload.php?group_id=177054). Fedora requires the Java SE Development Kit, available from Sun. Fedora allows the use of MySQL, Oracle, or Postgres. For a Web server, Fedora includes Apache Tomcat, but it also works with Jetty and JBoss.

It is important to understand that Fedora is not meant to be used as a standalone service. To maximize its usefulness, and to use it as an IR, it requires other components, which have to be developed onsite or taken from other sources. These include "authoring or ingest applications, search engines, workflow management, and security components such as user identity management" (Fedora Tutorial #1: Introduction to Fedora, 2008: 5). This obviously requires the services of a programmer—or many programmers—and is the main reason that so few institutions have implemented Fedora as a repository platform.

Structure and Administration

Fedora, as mentioned, requires additional components for administrative tasks and workflow management. The most popular of these is Fez, a front end to Fedora that was developed by the University of Queensland Library (see http://dev-repo.library.uq.edu.au/wiki/index.php/Main_Page). It uses PHP and MySQL. With Fez, administrators can be assigned and privileges granted. Access privileges to documents are assigned to the object. User groups can also be organized and access privileges assigned that way. In Fedora, documents are organized into collections, and collections are organized into communities.

Metadata

Fedora is OAI-PMH compatible, but this is only the beginning. It is the organization and representation of metadata that sets Fedora apart from other repository platforms. For Fedora does not simply supply fields for administrative, descriptive, and structural metadata; it creates *relationship metadata* and organizes it into a special database (Fedora Development Team, 2005). These relationships can be searched by and presented to users so that it is not just a search and retrieval system based on matching words; the relationships themselves between files or objects are searchable.

Support

Support for Fedora is problematic, partly because of the small number of implementers and partly because of the complexity of the system and, indeed, its flexibility. Institutions can and do use Fedora for different purposes, which may not always match the needs of any other institution. This leads to spotty support, as evidenced by the Official Fedora Commons FAQ, available at http://fedora-commons.org/confluence/display/FCKB/The+Official+Fedora+Commons+FAQ. This FAQ is part of the Fedora Commons wiki, the main source of support currently available for Fedora users. There are also user groups, and, as of 2008, a newsletter, also available from the wiki. Because of the need for other components to make Fedora into a functioning repository, support for those components (such as Fez) should also be evaluated. Any effort at implementation of Fedora should be expected to be self-sufficient.

BOTTOM LINE

Pros

The power and flexibility of Fedora have impressed everyone who has explored it (see, for example, Wyles, 2006), but few have gone on to implement it.

Cons

Fedora requires an extraordinary amount of technical support and significant upfront planning and development. There is little or no support available.

Commercial Platforms

Commercial platforms generally offer the ability to get a repository up and running faster than an open source implementation. They allow the institution to focus on filling the repository rather than dwelling on its structure and functionality. They provide some measure of peace of mind, with skilled technical staff responsible for servers, storage, and backup. For many institutions without sufficient technical support staff, they may be the best or even only option.

However, commercial platforms are always vulnerable to the changes of the marketplace, and, no matter how profitable and growing an enterprise may be or have been in the past, change can happen fast. It is incumbent on institutions using a commercial provider to have a plan for the delivery and storage of their data in case a transition to another platform becomes necessary. The vendor's role and responsibilities in this process should be clearly stated in any contract.

Other requirements for a contract include the terms governing technical support, backup procedures, the amount of storage allowed, costs for additional storage, and a list of participating sites (e.g., branch campuses).

Of course, the institution's own contract language requirements also need to be met, such as indemnifications, governing law, etc.

Digital Commons

For more information on Digital Commons, visit **www.bepress.com/ir**.

Digital Commons is a commercial platform offered by bepress. Bepress (Berkeley Electronic Press) was originally formed to create a journal publishing platform at the University of California, Berkeley, and indeed still produces dozens of journals. In partnership with the University of California system, bepress further developed its system to function as an IR platform, Digital Commons.

Implementation and Base Technology

Bepress has full responsibility for servers for Digital Commons repositories. This includes the live server as well as regular onsite and offsite backup. Bepress has a disaster recovery plan, and it is possible for institutions to receive regular delivery of their content for dark archiving. The only requirement for technical support from the institution is to add a line to the local DNS server (every institution has one) so that the URL of the repository can match that of the other units of the institution (such as siu.edu), but still point to the bepress servers.

Structure and Administration

Digital Commons' structure is similar to that of DSpace. Documents are collected into *series*, which are then placed under *communities*. Communities are typically departments, research centers, etc. Communities can have an unlimited number of subcommunities, and each community or subcommunity can have an unlimited number of series.

There are one or more *site administrators*, who have sole rights for requesting new communities and series from bepress, and only bepress staff can actually create the new communities and series. Each series can have one or more *series administrators* assigned, and these administrators have authority over posting documents to that series, as well as some control over the appearance of some basic interface features. This structure allows for a largely decentralized administration of the repository while still allowing tight control at the highest level.

Metadata

Digital Commons supports Dublin Core and is thus fully OAI-PMH compatible. Additional metadata fields can be added upon request; however, these fields are not searchable with the internal search tool. Metadata is exportable to RSS, XML, and bibliographic management utilities.

Support

Support is part of the deal when contracting for Digital Commons. Most importantly, technical support is entirely the responsibility of bepress. This does not mean that any and all requests are fulfilled, however. Digital Commons uses templates for every component of the repository, from the front page to individual communities, and help pages to journal configurations. Some customization is allowed, particularly institution branding, but in the end customers should be prepared to fulfill their users' needs with the standard templates. Turnaround time is not specified contractually; within 24 to 48 hours is typical, depending on the request. More detailed issues or requests may take significantly longer. Support is available via e-mail and telephone. Bepress conducts training sessions on administration and journal publication.

Bepress also provides support in the development of repository content, offering advice on best practices and onsite forums for the general user community. A Google Group is used for sharing questions, suggestions, and best practices among fellow Digital Commons institutions. Regular, informal user group meetings take place at American Library Association, Special Library Association, and other professional meetings.

Special Features

> To see the appearance of bepress journals, visit **www.bepress.com/journals/alljournals.html**.

The search tool allows for searching not just within the local repository but across all Digital Commons repositories. However, this feature works only with the simple search. Digital Commons provides for the complete administration of electronic journal publishing, including peer review.

Microsoft Word and RTF (rich text format) documents are converted automatically to PDFs. There is automatic notification of download statistics to authors via e-mail, and the statistics can be customized to some degree.

Price

Price is based on institution size. Bepress must be contacted for a quote. Negotiation has been possible, and it never hurts to try.

BOTTOM LINE

Pros

No onsite servers or technical support are required. There is a significant user community for advice and support. The journal publishing support is unique and well tested. A repository can be made live quickly. Regular automated delivery of download statistics to authors helps to sell the IR to contributors.

Cons

Digital Commons is not cheap. While institutional branding is easy, other customization seems to be increasingly discouraged and inflexible templates more common. Bepress formed a working partnership with ProQuest and benefited from the latter's extensive experience working with libraries. That partnership was severed in 2007. As with any commercial provider, there is always vulnerability to mergers and acquisitions.

CONTENTdm®

> For more information on CONTENTdm®, visit **www.contentdm.com**.

CONTENTdm® is a full asset management application, typically employed for an institution's entire set of digital collections, not just the IR. However, it was built for and works well only with images. A product of OCLC, it offers the benefits of years of development with close consultation with libraries.

Implementation and Base Technology

Content is stored either on the institution's own servers or on OCLC servers. The server can be Microsoft, Linux, or Sun, and the Web server can be Microsoft or Apache. It is a partially open system in that locally produced extensions can be implemented for the institution's instance. The interface can also be customized.

Structure and Administration

Items are organized into collections, but there are no separate series. Content is submitted through an Acquisition module, which requires installation on client computers. A separate Web interface is used for administering collections. Access restrictions are possible at the collection and item levels.

Metadata

Fields are completely customizable. CONTENTdm® is OAI-PMH compatible and also supports Dublin Core, Z39.50, and other standards. All metadata is encoded in XML, and XML is also supported for export to other applications. It is easy, for example, to batch load IR records into WorldCat. For those with a subscription to OCLC's Connexion client, it is possible to add the metadata created during cataloging directly into CONTENTdm® without the need for a separate entry process. Tab-delimited import, from Excel, for example, is supported. CONTENTdm® comes with *Library of Congress Thesaurus for Graphical Materials I.*

Support

OCLC provides Implementation Services to develop plans and provide tools to new institutions. An online User Support Center includes help files and tutorials, and there are regular meetings for user groups at library conferences. There is also a listserv and automatic notification of new developments for customers. Telephone and e-mail support are available.

Special Features

Image Rights tools simplify the identification of rights and ownership of content. An optional OCR extension converts image files of text into searchable text files.

Price

A number of options and support levels determine the price. The four license levels are based on the number of digital items to be included. Hosting services are optional. Licenses are also available for Development and Cold servers, for testing and emergency switchover, respectively. Because CONTENTdm® was developed as a digital collection management application, other options may be valuable in that role but are not strictly applicable to IR services.

BOTTOM LINE

Pros

The different licenses and hosting solutions make CONTENTdm® a flexible option. The large library user community is a plus. The tie-ins with other OCLC products and services add value for library implementers. For repositories with an emphasis on image files, there may be no better choice.

Cons

CONTENTdm® is priced as a digital collection management system. For those not already employing CONTENTdm®, it may be a prohibitively expensive option. The need for the acquisition software for submissions makes decentralized submission problematic. Creation and manipulation of the hierarchical structure are limited. While the ability to handle images is good, support for text and other content types has not been well developed.

DigiTool

Dawn Bastian-Paschal (Colorado State University) provided considerable help with the profile of DigiTool.

For more information on DigiTool, see **www.exlibrisgroup.com/category/DigiToolOverview**.

DigiTool is another digital asset management system, often used for digital collections beyond the typical IR. It is a product of Ex Libris and, as such, functions best with their integrated library system, Aleph. The ability to use this integrated library system, via the catalog, to access information within the repository is the strongest selling point of DigiTool. Information regarding the system is hard to come by except through formal channels with Ex Libris.

Implementation and Base Technology

DigiTool requires installation on the institution's servers, and all maintenance and backup and server support remain the responsibility of the institution. In this sense, it is a bit of a hybrid solution. DigiTool requires use of Apache Tomcat and Oracle and of Linux servers.

Structure and Administration

Content is organized into *collections* and *subcollections* rather than communities and series, as are other platforms. DigiTool uses a separate program for management services, which must be installed and updated on a user's computer. It allows multiple levels of administrative access.

Metadata

Dublin Core, MES, and EAD are all supported. DigiTool is OAI-PMH compliant. Meditor, the acquisition module, can be used for inputting metadata and is reported by some to be easy (Stevenson and Hodges, 2008), but its interface may be daunting to any who are not catalogers. It is also possible to use an XML template and load the XML file with the content. Adding new metadata fields is possible.

Support

Initial consultation is available for a fee. Training is available, both onsite and online, at a significant price. It provides a discussion list for paid customers.

Special Features

Using APIs (application programming interfaces), interaction is facilitated with other systems, including upload of data and content. For the user, the ability to sort contents by different fields, including subject, is valuable. Users can also store selected items in their individual spaces.

Price

DigiTool is more expensive than the other platforms. How expensive depends on the institution; quotes have to be solicited from Ex Libris. Costs include a license fee, setup fees, and maintenance fees. Initial consultation and training costs also have to be considered, as do the onsite servers. Pricing is also determined by the number of objects in the repository, so the more successful the repository, the more it costs, an unfortunate negative feedback loop.

BOTTOM LINE

Pros

Integration with the suite of Ex Libris products can be advantageous for some institutions. Customer support is good, though expensive. Batch loading is fast and efficient.

Cons

The price is high, and concerns of ownership and profits restrict sharing of information and experiences. There is no notification of download numbers and no support for individual faculty researcher pages.

Open Repository

Open Repository is a commercial platform offered by BioMed Central and has established some market share, particularly in the United Kingdom. There are no instances of Open Repository in the United States, but there are some sites in the United Kingdom and Europe; for those seeking a commercial service but unable to afford Digital Commons, CONTENTdm®, or DigiTool, it may be an option. However, its status is up in the air, because BioMed Central was acquired by Springer in 2008.

For more information on Open Repository, visit **www.openrepository.com.**

Implementation and Base Technology

Built on the DSpace software, Open Repository offers the gravitas of the most commonly employed platform without requiring the same level of onsite technical support. As with Digital Commons, all server space and maintenance are the responsibility of the vendor, as is backup and security. Open Repository charges for space beyond a limited amount, and the price is significant; exact pricing should be requested up front.

Structure, Administration, and Metadata

Structure, administration, and metadata are the same as those of a locally loaded instance of DSpace (see earlier description).

OTHER PLATFORMS

These platforms have shown some viability but do not have the track record of those examined in this chapter.

CDS Invenio
http://cdsware.cern.ch/invenio/index.html

ETD-db
http://scholar.lib.vt.edu/ETD-db/index.shtml

Greenstone
www.greenstone.org

VITAL
www.vtls.com/products/vital

Price

Two packages are available, and the price depends on the package selected. Each package requires a one-time setup fee and annual maintenance fees. The Standard Edition package includes technical support and some training support. The Silver Edition offers upfront batch uploading, automatic conversion of files to PDFs, authentication support, and data feeds from open access sources for automatic population of the IR. Pricing is available from the Open Repository site at www.openrepository.com/products. The prices listed include only minimal storage space.

BOTTOM LINE

Pros

DSpace has a large development network, which continuously improves the product. Implementation can be quick and painless and cheaper than most other platforms.

Cons

Although implementation can be done cheaply, additional space is quite expensive. Open Repository has a minimal track record and none in the United States.

Final Thoughts

Choosing a platform can be a make or break decision. Choosing open source without the technical support available may result in delays and disruptions in service, while choosing a commercial platform may result in unwelcome pressure to produce and produce early and often in order to justify the expense. The best strategy for finding the optimal solution for a given institution is to consult with other institutions of similar size and with similar goals and compare their experiences. While conferring with sales people or an insider and advocate of an open source platform will be necessary to get answers to all the necessary questions, they should not be the sole source of information for platform evaluations.

It is also important to assess the institution's level of risk aversion. Some of the more risky platforms—Fedora, for example—may have the most to offer. However, the final decision must rest on an honest appraisal of the institution's level of support—including budget, technical expertise, personnel, and philosophy—now and into the future. Finally, caution should be exercised when considering the importance of technical features, because it is not the technology that plays the crucial role in growing repositories. The quantity and quality of outreach are more determinative and deserve more attention.

References and Suggested Readings

Crow, Raym. 2002. "The Case for Institutional Repositories: A SPARC Position Paper." Available: www.arl.org/sparc/bm~doc/ir_final_release_102.pdf (accessed January 15, 2009).

Crow, Raym. 2004. "A Guide to Institutional Repository Software v 3.0." Available: www.soros.org/openaccess/software (accessed January 15, 2009).

Fedora Development Team. 2005. "Fedora Open Source Repository Software: White Paper." Available: www.fedora.info/pdfs/WhitePaper.10.28.05.pdf (accessed January 19, 2009).

"Fedora Tutorial #1: Introduction to Fedora." 2008. Available: http://fedora-commons.org/confluence/download/attachments/4718930/tutorial1.pdf?version=1 (accessed January 19, 2009).

Gibbons, Susan. 2004. "Institutional Repositories." *Library Technology Reports* 40, no. 4.

Marill, Jennifer, and Edward Luczak. "Evaluation of Digital Repository Software at the National Library of Medicine." *D-Lib Magazine* 9, no. 1. Available: www.dlib.org/dlib/may09/marill/05marill.html (accessed May 18, 2009).

"Repository Applications." *Library Technology Reports* 44, no. 2 (February 2008): 26–32.

Smith, MacKenzie, Mick Bass, Greg McClellan, and Robert Tansley. 2003. "DSpace: An Open Source Dynamic Digital Repository." *D-Lib Magazine* 9, no. 1. Available: www.dlib.org/dlib/january03/smith/01smith.html (accessed January 17, 2009).

Stevenson, Valerie, and Sue Hodges. 2008. "Setting up a University Digital Repository: Experience with DigiTool." *OCLC Systems & Services* 24, no. 1: 48–50.

Wheatley, Paul. 2004. "Institutional Repositories in the Context of Digital Preservation." *Microform & Imaging Review* 33, no. 3: 135–146.

Wyles, Richard, et al. 2006. "Technical Evaluation of Selected Open Source Repository Solutions, v1.3." Open Access Repositories in New Zealand (OARINZ) project, Christchurch Polytechnic Institute of Technology. Available: https://eduforge.org/docman/view.php/131/1062/Repository%20Evaluation%20Document.pdf (accessed January 15, 2009).

Policies and the Working Institutional Repository

4

Policy development is one of the more time-consuming aspects of repository implementation. Fortunately, once done, policies need be revisited and reworked only as needed. Even more fortunately, so many institutions have already developed their policies that it is possible to explore what is already out there and modify existing policies to fit local needs. This is one area where institutional repository (IR) managers can take advantage of pioneers' experiences.

IN THIS CHAPTER:

The Purposes of Policies

Policies serve multiple purposes (Probets and Jenkins, 2006). First and foremost, they provide a *structure* for IR staff to feel comfortable in. When dealing with a project of such a scale as IRs, which are often said to seek to capture "the intellectual output of the university" or other community, it is easy to become overwhelmed. Just determining what is "intellectual output" and what is the "community of contributors" are complex issues. By defining these parameters, it becomes easier to target certain members of the contributor pool, hone a successful message, and build a repository that is more than an extensive, very broad, but very shallow, collection. In addition, policies provide something to which staff can point in order to explain why they do or do not provide some service. In this regard, policies serve to protect IR staff in much the same way that traditional library collection development policies do.

> Simply search "repository policies" in your favorite search engine to get started.

Second, policies for public consumption serve as a way to deliver *information*, an easy way to describe the services offered by the IR and the conditions under which those services operate. They describe who can contribute and what they can contribute and what contributors' rights and responsibilities are. They also describe what the IR staff's rights and responsibilities are and what contributors can expect from the repository and its staff. A repository is a Web-based service for a Web-based world; policies provided online clarify what the repository is all

> See, for example, **http://opensiuc.lib.siu.edu/faq.html**.

about to those unknown users who can be directed to the site in a number of ways, intentional and serendipitous.

Policies Are Made to Be Broken

When developing policies, it is important to keep in mind the context of the IR as an innovative and often poorly understood service that is too often underutilized and underpopulated. Setting restrictions on who can contribute what can create order—but better a disordered collection of diversity than an ordered collection of nothing. Barriers to participation are counterproductive and may send a lasting message of noninclusion to crucial contributors and potential advocates. Policies may be a potential contributor's first exposure to the IR and therefore need to be crafted and administered to make that exposure a positive one.

Flexibility, the willingness to adapt the repository to the actual needs of researchers, may take the repository in unintended directions. This is not something to be avoided categorically. Ultimately, it is the community the IR is intended to serve that should decide just what it should be. Because, in the earlier stages, the community will be largely ignorant of what the IR is, it is unrealistic to expect the community to make significant contributions to policy development at the time of implementation. This is why, at this stage, limiting the IR via policies will help concentrate focus and, especially, ensure manageability. Such restrictions are understandable, even recommended; but they should not be inviolable.

Policies

The minimal policies that need to be developed cover the following:

- Establishing communities and collections
- Administering the IR communities
- Contributors
- Content types, file formats, and versioning
- Use of content
- Submission agreements
- Submission process
- Withdrawal and retention
- Preservation efforts

Establishing Communities and Collections

Repositories are organized into communities and subcommunities. In the academic setting, a community is typically a college, school, or department or a research center or institute, although other communities can and do exist. Each community or subcommunity can then have one or more collections or series. How and by whom they are created is one of the first decisions that need to be made.

A policy regarding the establishment of new communities and collections should not require the agreement or acceptance by all members of a particular community. Willingness to participate by one member of the community should suffice to get the ball rolling. If, on the other hand, a requirement is made that departmental approval must be secured before the establishment of a community and its collections, delay and even refusal may result. It is important, however, to establish who within the community can initiate a new IR presence: for an academic institution, faculty may be the best choice as the only designated members who can do so. This will provide a sense of control over structure and quality, which some will need in order to feel comfortable. If students are allowed to initiate a community and collections, faculty may see the service as too open and not providing the kind of authority they naturally want their work to have.

Administering the IR Communities

Even after having established the staffing for the IR, delegation of responsibilities and rights is not finished. Allocating some administrative responsibilities to a variety of people in the institution is common, sensible, and even desirable. Regardless of platform, IRs are divided into communities and collections, each of which requires an administrator. Communities are typically academic or governing units. Collections are aggregations of documents based on some common feature or function, such as technical reports, journal articles, and conference proceedings. It is possible to have hundreds of communities and subcommunities and even more collections. Assigning administrator status to some of these can help ease the burden while still allowing IR staff to maintain overall control.

Administration of collections is not overly demanding from a technical point of view. It does require time, however, and also a grasp of IR policies. Distributing responsibility will certainly require time on the part of IR staff to train administrators and provide support to them. In terms of policies, it requires the determination of who will be allowed to fill this role and what independence they will be granted in carrying out that role.

Determining who can be an administrator is a discretionary decision of IR staff, because all necessary skill requirements can be taught within an hour or two and are within the capabilities of almost anyone in an academic institution. However, IR staff have to be comfortable with these administrators, as they will have to work with them on a regular basis, and they will have to trust the administrators to enforce the policies of the IR. It may be advisable to begin with faculty and staff, monitor the results, and open things up to students as the need develops.

It is also important to have an understanding, before training of administrators begins, of how much authority they will be given to adjust policies, further delegate responsibility, conduct additional training, and, in general, make decisions regarding their particular community and collections. The easiest and best policy is to require adherence to the IR policies and to seek permission from IR staff before changing them. This, in combination with an open mind when it comes to requested modifications, should satisfy diverse institutional needs while maintaining an appropriate level of control. This is particularly important when copyright and other legal issues are in play, and the IR staff assume ultimate legal responsibility. Should this requirement for consultation become unwieldy for a given community, staff hold on the reins can be loosened.

Contributors

Every IR has a defined circle of possible contributors (*the contributor pool*). One reason for this is the sheer magnitude of operating a repository in any other way, essentially beyond the capability of the resources most institutions are willing or able to commit to the service. Commercial providers restrict the contributor pool to an institution or, in some cases, a consortium for the same reason and in order to preserve future sales. If one institution serves as the repository for a number of others, those others would have no need to contract with the commercial provider. For the same reason, providers may restrict the use of their software to a single site, although this is usually negotiable.

Faculty

In an academic setting, all faculty will be part of the contributor pool. They are creating the research and other intellectual output that have a demonstrated demand and that have been for so long distributed in the traditional scholarly communication system. It is the prospective and increasing failure of this system to meet the needs of so many that inspired open access efforts—including IRs—to begin with. Therefore, all faculty should be considered as legitimate contributors to the IR.

> Even adjunct or temporary faculty can be included in an IR, and no distinction need be made between them and other faculty.

Outside of faculty, policies will differ by institution. Keeping in mind, as always, the context of underutilized, underpopulated IRs, there will be local reasons for allowing or disallowing other constituents—staff and students, in the academic setting—to participate.

Staff

Staff may be responsible for any number of content types that might be targeted for inclusion in the IR. These can include newsletters, which may be produced by many or all departments or units, public relations pieces, operating documents (such as committee reports or meeting minutes), data (such as is generated for accreditation efforts), and more. To the extent that these types of material are allowed in the IR, it may be necessary to allow the staff who produce them to join the contributor pool.

Students

Two issues need to be considered regarding graduate and undergraduate contributions. One is the *quality* of the content, which by its nature may be deemed to be inferior when compared to faculty contributions (Pickton and McKnight, 2007). One content type commonly developed is a collection of theses and dissertations (see Chapter 6), documents which are generally viewed as being at an acceptably high enough level of quality to merit inclusion. However, this may be the only material that is allowed from graduate students.

Restrictions on undergraduate work will normally be tighter. While honor's theses—almost always from seniors—may be allowed, other undergraduate contributions are often prohibited. Given the idea of the repository as a recruiting tool for the institution, the institution is poorly served if the content does not reach an acceptable standard, and much undergraduate work does not. Another factor is the sheer *quantity* of student work—term papers, book reports, etc. Reviewing this amount of content is essentially impossible for an IR staff. For these reasons, student work is often left out.

However, there are advantages to including such work. Most student work, particularly at the undergraduate level, is not intended for publication—so the whole issue of copyright and the impact of prior publication do not apply. This means an easier path to gathering content. Additionally, exposing students to the concept of open access at this stage of their careers may pay dividends down the road. Discussing open access and IRs almost always will include some discussion of scholarly communication in general, and these discussions are hard to get teaching moments for. Students exposed to repositories now may be more inclined to use them as they themselves become research faculty, looking to disseminate their research. Finally, if the content is at an acceptable level, or offers some unique aspect, student work may contribute to the recruitment role of the IR. Prospective students may be attracted by an undergraduate poetry journal, for example.

Contributors from Outside the Institution

It may seem contradictory to have IR contributions from individuals who are not part of the institution, but there are reasons to allow them, and it is often done. These contributions can be from outside authors, speakers, artists, etc., who contribute to an institutionally sponsored event or publication. Conferences or seminar series with well-known speakers, or perhaps locally run journals with renowned authors, are an attractive addition to the IR, bringing attention beyond the normal scope of the institution. Commercial IR platform providers always allow inclusion of this type of noninstitutional contribution; language indicating this should be part of any signed agreement.

Content Types

IRs can be and are different things to different people or institutions. The types of content that can be included in an IR can be as diverse as the institution feels appropriate. Defining the content allowed from the beginning can help prevent "mission creep," the trend to expand the original intent of the IR to include all sorts of content and services. For an IR with a small staff, this can be essential. Spending time on projects outside the scope of the original mission means less time spent on that mission. This is one factor that leads to broad but shallow collections, a pervasive problem.

The primary determination that needs to be made from the start is whether only scholarly content will be collected or whether nonscholarly content will also be allowed. Scholarly content would, in this sense, essentially be equivalent to peer-reviewed content, such as journal articles, book chapters, and refereed conference presentations and publications. Restricting content to scholarly work has its advantages, as it is a simple way to guarantee an acceptable level of quality, and it protects and enhances the institution's reputation and status.

Also, restricting the content allowed, such as to scholarly material only, can help IR staff to focus on the types of content that will best serve to market the IR to more contributors. To some extent this will depend on the pool of contributors identified in the contributor policies. So, if faculty, particularly research faculty, are the primary target for the IR, it does not make much sense to start off the IR with a push to gather as many institutional records as possible. Researchers will be impressed more by other researchers' contributions to and experience with the IR.

Remembering the real-world context, however, it is inadvisable to overly restrict content type. For one thing, there are connections among any institution's staff, unknown to the IR staff, and even two apparently disparate departments or offices may have unseen networks that can lead to information dissemination about the IR. Working with any constituency to solve some institutional, technological need will generate goodwill that can be called upon later. Entree is essential in IR work, and working with departmental staff on something as mundane as posting meeting minutes can provide that entree.

Furthermore, meeting minutes and other archival records may be determined to be a legitimate source of content for the IR. An important function of an IR is to be a reliable preservation resource, and most institutions will be required to make a preservation commitment for many of their operational documents. IRs can serve that function and help to organize it into searchable form as well. There is no reason to shun this type of content outright in favor of scholarly research, which is often the primary content target for IRs (at least in the academic setting). In fact, there is a wealth of such "gray literature" that can be collected. IRs tend to develop lives of their own, and this is one of the more promising and interesting aspects they present. It is impossible to predict where they will fit in the information dissemination landscape in 20 years, and staff should do what they can to promote them as part of that landscape. Choking off their growth because of preconceived notions of what they should or should not do is unwise.

As a reaction to increasingly prohibitively expensive traditional scholarly communication, managers of IRs have targeted scholarly research as potential content of the first order, i.e., research that is either still intended for publishing in a journal or previously would have been. This goes to the heart of the reason for IRs—increased access to the research for all those individuals and institutions who cannot afford to pay for the standard delivery vehicle—typically a journal. Indeed, the original developers of IRs had this exactly in mind (Lynch, 2003).

Scholarly research certainly does receive increased use when made available via open access, including in IRs (Lawrence, 2001). This may be particularly true for researchers in developing countries, who do not have the library collections or library services, such as interlibrary loan, to deliver the content they need. This extended reach is a sufficient reason to target published or publishable research as IR content.

Copyright becomes a major issue for scholarly research. It is discussed in detail in Chapter 6.

File Formats

Most IR platforms can support all file types, because, at its rawest, a repository is simply a server, and servers can store any digital file type. But there may be reasons to restrict the file types that a repository will support.

Not all file types are created equal. Some consume more space than others. When initially planning for an IR, this may not seem like an issue, given the relatively inexpensive cost of servers. Even the commercial providers who charge for storage beyond some negotiated amount may seem to be offering more than will ever be used.

File formats supported by DSpace can be found at **http://libraries.mit.edu/dspace-mit/build/policies/format.html**.

But certain files will quickly push the original estimates. This is particularly true for multimedia files—especially in archival format. In addition, it can be difficult to predict all of the actual uses for the IR at the beginning, as the institution's members may have ideas of their own of ways to use it—ways that are not easily determined beforehand by a survey. To avoid either having to spend more than what is originally budgeted for more space or being embarrassed by turning down submissions because of a lack of space, it may be advisable to restrict file types from the start. If space and bandwidth are beyond an institution's means, or if the commercial provider's charges for expanded space are prohibitive, restrictions on files—multimedia files in particular, especially video files—may be necessary.

Versioning

It is possible in any repository to maintain any number of versions of a document. This may be desirable to demonstrate the history of a document and the ideas behind it. Replacement of existing files may be restricted in order to protect the stated commitment to permanence of deposited content. If multiple versions are allowed, a policy should state which versions will be presented to the world and in what context. Space limitations may come into play here, and an institution may wish to restrict all documents to a single version.

Use of Content

The whole raison d'être for an IR is to provide open access to a variety of content types. Nevertheless, how that content can be used may vary by type, by author, and by repository. Here again, a general rule should be established for internal and external informational purposes to achieve clarity and to maintain a unified purpose. However, inflexible adherence to this rule is counterproductive and unnecessary.

A usage policy should indicate that, first and foremost, the authors of the contents retain copyright (assuming they had it to begin with), and any use beyond those defined on the site may be restricted and must be approved by those authors. This has the benefit of assuaging the concerns of tenure and promotion track researchers or anyone else who wants to hold on to the copyright for financial or other reasons, thereby making them more likely to participate.

Typically, the uses allowed for repository content include the right to *view*, *print*, and *download* it. Further rights may include the right to distribute the content, provided it is done without accepting money for doing so. For most content, these rights should be granted at a minimum, and a policy should state this clearly. The policy should also indicate that proper attribution and citation are required as for any other resource, print or electronic.

Restricted Access

Sometimes, the repository might be used by a small, defined community for the purpose of sharing content that is being worked on by individual members. The community may want this content to be hidden from everyone else, at least until it is completed. Furthermore, authors may be prevented from making content available for a certain period of time to satisfy funder or publisher demands but yet still want to make available the metadata associated with the files. Theses and dissertations may also require restricted access in case of concerns about future publication, patents, or other intellectual property issues.

In these cases, the usage rights typically granted are not appropriate. In most repositories, limiting usage rights can be achieved by restricting access to the content to a defined user community, determined by traditional techniques such as e-mail domain or IP address. All of the major platforms allow for this kind of restriction. A policy needs to state that these exceptions may occur.

Creative Commons and User Rights

For more information on Creative Commons, visit **http://creativecommons.org**.

Science Commons, a project of Creative Commons, works similarly to address the specific needs of scientists. See **http://sciencecommons.org**.

Recent developments allow for even more sophisticated designation of rights for the user. It is possible to insert a Creative Commons license for any repository content. These licenses are easy to create and incorporate into a document's access point in the repository. Creative Commons licenses can include any or all of the following: *attribution*, which essentially allows for any use, even commercial, provided credit to the author is given; *attribution share-alike*, allowing the same rights but requiring that any new work based on the author's must have the same license terms; and *attribution no-derivatives*, which allows the same uses as the above except that no modification can be made to the original. Each of these can further be modified by restricting use to *noncommercial uses* only. Once an author selects the license desired, he or she simply clicks on a link, and the necessary html coding, ready for insertion where appropriate, is provided.

All this assumes that the author retains the copyright to the original work. For published works, this may not be the case. In this case, what users can do with the content is determined by the publisher. Chapter 6 presents information on resources and methods for identifying publisher policies.

Submissions

When considering policies for submissions, protection needs to be offered to contributors, to ensure their participation, and to IR staff and the institution, to ensure protection from violations of the law. Both of these protections are provided via submission agreements. Submissions also require a working policy regarding who will perform the actual submissions. The chosen policy will have implications for workload and workflow.

Submission Agreements

Submission agreements are an essential component of the repository service. They represent a way to clearly establish what the institution can do with the submissions and what rights are reserved to the author. They provide a measure of protection to the repository staff, as any challenges to the actions or functions of the IR concerning a particular document can be answered by the author's prior acceptance of the submission agreement. For this to be the case, authors must be made aware of the agreement and indicate their acceptance in some fashion.

There are varied ways of accomplishing this. Some institutions require a paper copy be signed and returned to the repository staff. This was more common in the early days of repository implementation, when there were fewer precedents to point to and caution ran high. However, it is the most difficult and time-consuming to administer, as it requires the delivery and return of a paper document. These then must be stored and preserved. To make them useful, either they need to be scanned or a list of author names needs to be maintained so that there is not a lengthy process involved to check the paper files for every submission to see if an agreement is on hand for the given author. This method may still be necessary in some states or countries where electronic signatures or click-through agreements are not accepted as legally binding. It is necessary to check with the appropriate legal authorities to determine this.

Click-through agreements are far easier to use. Authors are simply asked to acknowledge the terms established at the time of the submission, usually before the submission is even started. Because no submission is allowed without the agreement being accepted, no internal tracking of author names is necessary. If such agreements are allowable under law, they are the preferred method.

However, click-throughs will only work when the author and the submitter are one and the same. Often, this is not the case; submissions are done by a designated person in the department, center, or other community or by the IR staff. In this case, notification to and acceptance by the author of the terms of the agreement is still necessary. The indication of acceptance can be implicit in the act of submission; authors can be told that, by submitting, they agree to be bound by the terms of the submission agreement. Or, a more cautious approach can be taken, with written or electronic (i.e., e-mail) acceptance required. This approach again requires the tracking of agreements by the author.

As always, the real-world context of IRs needs to be taken into consideration. What works best for most contributors, and least restricts participation, provided all necessary protections are in place, is the important policy driver. Submission agreements come with the territory, but they should not deter involvement. Paper agreements in particular represent an obstacle to participation.

What Needs to Be in an Agreement?

The only absolutes that must be in an agreement are that the author gives the repository a nonexclusive right to distribute the submission in electronic format in perpetuity and that the author actually maintains the copyright in order to do so or has the permission of the copyright holder to do so. This simple statement covers almost all contingencies faced by repository staff and is all that a repository needs in order to function.

The nonexclusion component is necessary for two reasons. First, the work may already be or is intended to be published elsewhere. This is one reason why no copyright is turned over to the repository or its managers. Second, no authors are going to sign away their rights entirely for the repository to act as sole distributor of their content. The current reward systems, financial and professional, prohibitively discourage such an action.

The two essential aspects of nonexclusion are format and duration. It is important to indicate that the repository will have the right to distribute the material in any format, because it is unknowable what formats may predominate in the future. If migration to a new format becomes necessary, as should be expected, it will be unworkable to retrospectively gather the permission of contributors to make available their contributions in this new format.

This should not represent a significant concern for authors, because it is made clear to them from the start that one of the goals of the repository is to preserve the content forever. This aspect, too, should be included in the agreement—that the repository reserves the right to make the content available in perpetuity.

The copyright issue is thornier. It is incumbent on repository staff to attempt to verify copyright status for repository content. This may be easier when repository staff are doing the submissions themselves or are acting as editors or administrators of a given collection, where their approval is required before any content is actually posted. This may not always be the case, because some repositories allow direct submissions and decentralized administration. Indeed, as discussed above, this may be the preferred model for an institution with minimal staffing assigned to the IR. This is why the burden is, and should be, placed on the author to acknowledge that he or she has the copyright, or the agreement of the copyright holder, to post the content.

In practice, IR staff can and usually do work with authors to determine the copyright status of something already published. While sensible and practical for the beginning stages, this could be unworkable in the long term if the repository ever achieves the optimistic goal of acquiring the majority or even all of an institution's research output. To take some of the burden off of repository staff, the submission agreement should stress the author's responsibility to know the status of the copyrights for the works they have produced. As a side benefit, once they are exposed to this language, at least some authors will pay more attention to the publisher agreements that they sign. The submission agreement can be and has been used as a wedge to get authors to pay closer attention and even to attempt to use an agreement addendum stating that authors retain the right to post the document in a repository (among other things).

Acknowledgment of copyright ownership, or permission of the copyright holder to deposit, is essential for the reasons described. The agreement should also state that the contributor confirms that the contribution does not violate anyone else's copyright. It is not just imperative to clear the copyright status of the contribution itself but also the contents of that contribution. Repository liability can be limited by the use of such terms in the agreement.

This confirmation of copyright clearance is typically bundled with other acknowledgments of the contributor, including that the contribution does not violate proprietary rights, contain any libelous material, or violate any privacy rights. Individual institutions may require additional language, which is why it is important to have this cleared by legal counsel. A final element is a catch-all confirmation that the contribution does not violate any other repository policies. This may provide an escape clause for the repository administrators should one become necessary.

The less complicated the language, the less intimidating (and perhaps discouraging) it will be for the contributor pool. A typical agreement should read something like what is shown in the sidebar.

The Author's Rights

The repository too should have a policy specifying the author's rights beyond that implied in the nonexclusive component of the agreement. Specifically, it should be made clear that the repository does not assume any copyright, only the distribution right contained in the submission agreement. In some repositories, this language is included in the submission agreement itself; elsewhere, it is listed separately.

The Submission Process

Policies on submissions involve more than the rights maintained or granted by the author to the repository owners. Who can make the submissions and the required metadata are two of the most common elements in such a policy.

The two general models for submissions are self-submission and mediated submission. Often, it is the realities on the ground that determine which will be used rather than a theoretical framework. This is because when dealing with busy potential contributors, involvement

EXAMPLE OF AGREEMENT BETWEEN AUTHOR AND IR

I hold the copyright to this document and grant permission for posting it in the (blank) IR, or have the approval of the copyright holder to do so, and agree that it may be made available to the public in any format in perpetuity.

I warrant that the posting of the work does not infringe any copyright, nor violate any proprietary rights, nor contain any libelous matter, nor invade the privacy of any person or third party, nor otherwise violate Repository policies.

may be procured only by having IR staff do most of the work, including submission. Nevertheless, a decentralized model is often the goal for an already overworked staff, so self-submission should be a possibility, if not a requirement. A policy on submission should include the possibility of either self- or mediated submissions; repository staff should hope for the former and expect to do the latter.

Metadata

A policy on metadata is also needed. There is no question that more and better metadata enhance content discovery. Some institutions require a significant amount of metadata, with many current and future applications in mind. Concerns about versioning, supplementary files being linked together, etc., lead them to require considerable descriptive and/or administrative metadata. Certainly, this is the ideal path.

Each institution will have to decide how far down that path it wants to go. Given that most IR content is indexed by search engines, and that this is how most users find the content, discoverability may not be as metadata dependent as traditional resources, particularly for a repository with a preponderance of full-text documents, which is usually the case. Additionally, requiring extensive metadata, from either the author or the administrator, is a barrier to participation. For authors, it requires more of a time commitment than most people are willing to give—to learn the fields, format, etc. Author, title, date, and perhaps an abstract and keywords may be all they are willing to do. This may also be all that administrators have time to do. Again, policies need to be driven by real-world conditions, with a goal toward maximizing involvement. Metadata is discussed further in Chapter 7.

Withdrawal and Retention

Getting involvement is a significant achievement. Once submissions have been made, it is important to try to keep them. This is why most repositories have a policy of not allowing withdrawals except under some very specific circumstances. These usually are because of legal concerns and can include copyright infringement, libelous content, violation of privacy, etc. Otherwise, withdrawal should be discouraged. With a delicate hold on the information communication landscape, IRs need to be reliable if they are to be seen as serious and worthy places to disseminate information. Fluctuating content damages that potential. Nevertheless, there may be circumstances when allowing withdrawal is actually the more politic decision. Goodwill is needed as well as reliability, so a policy on withdrawal and retention should simply state that withdrawal is heavily discouraged but allowable under some circumstances, and repository staff should be contacted for any particular case.

Preservation

Preservation is one of the library's charges, which is why it makes sense for libraries to be actively involved in repositories. It is simply an extension of the library's traditional role into the electronic realm, serving as the institution's or community's memory and bringing that role up to date.

But digital preservation involves different skills and knowledge than preservation of physical volumes. It is a topic beyond the scope of this work except to say that repository policies need to account for this tricky issue. After all, this is one of the selling points, that material will continue to be available, offering a degree of stability not present with an individual's or department's Web page.

How this is stated in a policy is varied. One basic commitment, fairly easy to meet, is that all content is backed up so that the repository server is not the sole source of the content. Commercial vendors will provide this service themselves; repositories maintained onsite will have to provide backup themselves. One simple component of a preservation policy is that preservation is easier to commit to for nonproprietary formats (RTF files as opposed to Microsoft Word files, for example), and for this reason these formats are favored.

In truth, it is not possible to positively guarantee the preservation of any or all electronic files, at least in usable form. Files require some sort of reader or player, or other software, to make them usable. It is impossible to state that there will always be such software for any particular file format. Thus, while a commitment can be made to preserve the file itself, its functioning is, and always will be, at a greater or lesser risk. Libraries can, however, describe these levels of risk. Many IRs are using a chart first described by the developers at MIT, which lists various format types, and then indicates the level of support offered by the repository: Supported, Known, or Not Supported (see http://libraries.mit.edu/dspace-mit/build/policies/format.html). However, even a rating of Supported is conditional and can offer only a higher likelihood of continuing functionality.

Additional Policies

The policies discussed thus far are the minimal policies necessary to run a repository. However, some institutions will want to consider implementing other policies, given particular circumstances.

Fees for Space

For those IRs providing the storage space themselves, and for those using a commercial platform whose vendor charges for space above a certain amount, it may be necessary to establish maximum space allotments for a community beyond which fees are assessed. However, if the maximum is too low, it will discourage participation, as departments will likely be unable or unwilling to commit financial resources to the repository, especially in its early stages. If fees are necessary beyond low storage maximums, the platform selection and/or the decision to pursue an IR need to be reevaluated.

Commercial Uses

Two circumstances might need to be addressed regarding commercial uses. The first is the institution's commercial use of the author-deposited content, including the metadata. The second is commercial use by individual authors, departments, or other units for their own work. Bepress' Digital Commons, which supports a variety of functions involved in journal publishing, may especially present the opportunity to sell content served through the repository, but other platforms may do so as well. This will require a whole set of support services, so staff will have to determine whether they have the infrastructure to provide commercial use. Philosophical issues may also help to determine policy on this issue. In both circumstances, it should be clearly spelled out under what terms and situations commercial uses are allowed and what rights are retained by all parties.

Privacy

Privacy is an issue for repositories that collect personal information during the submission process and for repositories providing alerting services. Privacy policies will have to comply with terms established by the institution as a whole, and little choice will be available to repository staff. Legal counsel for the institution must be consulted.

Legal Aspects

Most of the policies described in this chapter are internal working guidelines, which do not carry the force of the law behind them. They are strictly a framework within which it is easier, more convenient, and more comfortable for IR administrators to operate and contributors to participate. As such, they are not decisions that need be subject to review from legal counsel or upper administration.

However, some of the policies are legally binding, and due diligence requires that they have the approval of the necessary authorities. This includes the language of the submission agreement, which all contributors are required to either sign, agree to via a click-through agreement, or otherwise acknowledge being bound to. Although the language may be standard and seemingly innocuous, local rules may vary, and, if enforcement becomes necessary at some point (however unlikely this may seem), it is the legal authority that will be required to seek it. It is inappropriate to tie this legal authority's hands by an agreement that they have never reviewed. Privacy rules are also legally binding. Similarly, monitoring the copyright status of submissions has legal implications, and it should be clear, among both IR staff and any designated administrators of communities or collections, who has this responsibility. All policies regarding these issues should be reviewed by a legal expert before implementation, and they should be clearly stated on the repository site.

References

Lawrence, Steve. 2001. "Online or Invisible?" *Nature* 411, no. 6837: 521.

Lynch, Clifford. 2003. "Institutional Repositories: Essential Infrastructure for Scholarship in the Digital Age." *portal: Libraries and the Academy* 3, no. 2: 327–336.

Pickton, Margaret and Cliff McKnight. 2007. "Is There a Role for Research Students in an Institutional Repository? Some Repository Managers' Views." *Journal of Librarianship & Information Science* 39, no. 3: 153–161.

Probets, Steve and Celia Jenkins. 2006. "Documentation for Institutional Repositories." *Learned Publishing* 19, no. 1: 57–71.

Marketing and Recruitment for the Institutional Repository

5

IN THIS CHAPTER:

The most common complaint about repositories is that there is not enough in them. They may represent a significant commitment from an institution—in terms of staffing and funding—and yet be underutilized. While there are many examples of very successful institutional repositories (IRs), the fact remains that most of them have failed to achieve the goals set out for them, and many are embarrassingly thin.

Know Your Audience

Addressing this gap between expectation and reality requires a multipronged effort. These efforts must get underway even before the IR is rolled out, particularly with regard to a marketing plan. A marketing plan includes two aspects: crafting a message and finding the best ways to deliver it. To be effective, both aspects must take into account the audience's habits and preferences.

A well-crafted message is one that is designed to appeal to the identifiable and recognized needs of the community. Each community can be subdivided into subcommunities, and no one message is going to resonate the same with each and every subcommunity. A well-crafted marketing plan, therefore, will take into consideration these different subcommunities and will include a set of messages, which can be cherry-picked from as needed for any particular audience.

The first step, then, in designing a marketing plan is to know your audience. This can be accomplished in a couple of ways: via a formal assessment of some sort, most likely a survey, or, more informally, through communication channels that are a regular function within the institution and have already been in place for some time. The two are not exclusive, and what works for one institution may not work for another.

Surveys

An assessment plan usually involves a survey, designed to gather information on the needs of the community and its perception of

An example of a faculty survey is the University of Massachusetts' at **http://works.bepress.com/cgi/viewcontent.cgi?article=1020&context=marilyn_billings.**

the IR service. Some typical questions in such a survey include the following:

- What types of files do you create as part of your occupation (research and teaching)?
- How and where do you store these files?
- How and with whom do you share them?
- How do you locate and retrieve others' research?

Surveys can help to establish which aspects of the IR most closely match the needs of the contributor pool. If properly designed, they can identify unanticipated areas where the IR can be beneficial. They can also reduce the design and use of poorly crafted marketing tools by indicating which aspects of the IR do *not* appeal to the contributor pool. This may be the most useful benefit of a survey, as the benefits of an IR that seem obvious or most important to the librarian (or whoever is responsible for delivering the message) may not be important or relevant to the contributor pool. Filtering out these preconceptions can save time. Because IR staff will often have a limited time to deliver the message, each component of that message, and each minute, must count. A survey can help in honing the message accordingly.

Surveys do have drawbacks. First, it takes time to design and administer them and to compile the results. Second, achieving any sort of reasonable response rate is a challenge difficult to overcome, and this has significant consequences. Because different members of the institution, particularly in an academic institution, have diverse means of communicating research results and other information, survey results from one subcommunity will not necessarily reflect an accurate picture of other subcommunities. Inferences from partial survey responses have to be applied cautiously, and a survey is no substitute for doing the harder, more time-intensive work of investigation into each individual's output and communication methods and conducting one-on-one discussions.

Other Assessment Techniques

This harder and more time-intensive work may not require significant additional effort for an academic library, because the work is already a normal part of the daily workload of subject liaisons. They already have as an area of their responsibility an awareness of the communication methods of their constituencies. They are already monitoring Web pages, journal and book publications, lecture or seminar series, etc., for the departments assigned to them. They may even attend thesis and dissertation defenses and thus learn the research techniques of graduate students. In fact, there are many ways for liaisons to gain an understanding of research communication in academic departments, and it is incumbent on them to do so. This understanding then can be brought to bear on the development of the IR, which must be considered a reflexive service designed to accommodate the different needs of different communities and subcommunities (Jenkins, Breakstone, and Hixson, 2005).

There is another way to develop knowledge about contributor needs, and this informal survey method should not be overlooked as a source of information either. Marketing the IR, by going out to departments to raise awareness of it, raises the possibility of directly gathering information from faculty without requiring them to fill out any forms. Offering potential contributors the chance to suggest uses for the IR, during any and every presentation or discussion about it, functions as a survey by allowing direct input from those with real and unmet communication, storage, and management needs. Each presentation should be a two-way discussion, not merely an announcement of what the IR is for.

Content of the Message

Think of the preparation of a message as a preparation of a smorgasbord, where you can pick out the pieces that are of most use for the audience at hand. This is necessary because, unless your institution is a homogenous one, its members will have different methods of communication, different styles of conducting and sharing research, and different technological needs.

While general messages to the entire community may incorporate many or all of the elements relating to the benefits of an IR, eventually discussions will devolve to a smaller scale, perhaps a department, most likely an individual. For these discussions, the scattershot approach is inadequate, and the message needs to be more sharply honed. This is where picking from a complete menu of ideas becomes necessary.

What are these menu items, the elements of a marketing message? They will include the following:

- What an IR is
- Why the institution is running one
- What the benefits are and why the individual should contribute
- How to proceed

What an IR Is

The first element in any message is a description of the IR. Although most will be familiar with the concept of an online archive, understanding of how one works and how it is managed may be minimal. It is therefore necessary to define and describe IRs in terms that the audience can understand. This definition does not have to reflect the entire spectrum of issues concerning the software, hardware, laws, finances, etc., which the managers will have to grapple with before reaching this stage. A definition of "institutional repository" for public consumption is just a tool for conveying quickly what is being offered to, and asked of, the audience.

"Institutional Repository"

There is widespread recognition that the term "institutional repository" is somewhat clumsy and uninspiring. While it is no doubt recognizable for the majority of academic librarians and many information technologists, its spread outside of those communities is negligible. There are reasons to use it when marketing—most prominent is that there simply is nothing better—but it is by itself insufficient to achieve common understanding with the audience. Each institution will have to decide for itself, but it may be advantageous to avoid the term altogether. Some use "electronic archive," or just "archive," in its stead; many in the community who are unfamiliar with the IR will think of it as a "database"; some managers simply refer to the name and avoid any terminology at all. For this reason, it is important to come up with a creative and memorable name. It is important also to use the name as a branding opportunity and to use the institution's name in the name of the IR; e.g., OpenSIUC, DigitalCommons@Wayne State University, UR Research (for the University of Rochester), etc.

However, it is inevitable that discussion of similar services at other institutions will be mentioned, because a local IR is part of a larger effort to expand access to information by creating hundreds or thousands of IRs, so some generic appellation should be decided upon at an early date. To avoid confusion, all staff associated with the IR should be encouraged to use this agreed upon term, whatever it is, and all formal communications should adopt it.

One of the most common definitions of an IR is Clifford Lynch's; although first used for a university IR, it is broad enough that it transfers to other environments as well:

> [A] university-based institutional repository is a set of services that a university offers to the members of its community for the management and dissemination of digital materials created by the institution and its community members. It is most essentially an organizational commitment to the stewardship of these digital materials, including long-term preservation where appropriate, as well as organization and access or distribution. (Lynch, 2003)

This definition gets to the heart of the matter quickly and concisely. It is still, however, not couched in user-friendly language and is best suited for an audience actively seeking to learn more about an IR, not necessarily one that has little time or inclination to listen to a one-hour spiel. For this latter type of audience, an even more concise definition will be more to the point:

"An IR is an electronic archive of the intellectual output of an institution." Or even more concisely: "An IR is a place to put stuff."

Beyond the Terminology

Regardless of the definition used, explaining what an IR is will need to include some further elements, namely, the essential elements described in Chapter 4, the chapter on policies. Not everything need be included at this stage, as the marketing stage is presumed to be followed by more in-depth discussions when the target audience or a member thereof agrees to participate. At that time, more detailed explanations can be given. At this point, it is necessary to include just a few elements:

- Who can contribute?
- What types of material can be contributed?
- What happens to the contributions once they are in the IR?

Realistically, answering these three questions will provide enough information for the audience to grasp what the IR is. The answers will have to be institution specific so that bland generalities will be avoided. The questions are to the point, so the audience will know immediately if they personally are included and if the message needs to be shared with anyone else (e.g., staff and students) in order to secure their involvement. It should also be reasonably clear to them whether any ideas that come to mind for potential contribution are or are not possible. However, flexibility in all of these areas should also be stressed, because this stage is too early to be ruling out anything.

Why the Institution Is Running One

This element is the bridge between the questions of what an IR is and why individuals should contribute to it. It provides the opportunity to talk about the information communication landscape and its deficiencies. Answering this question allows discussion of issues that may not be important to individuals, or that they do not normally think about, but that are important for the institution as a whole. For example, many are using IRs as marketing tools for the institution, recruitment tools to increase enrollment, attract candidates, raise status, etc. While for many individuals this will not be a priority, it may be for department heads or other administrators. To a greater or lesser extent, this interest then makes it important for the individuals as well.

Also, declining local resources, especially in the library, do have an impact. Younger researchers will be concerned about exposure and the ability to acquire new resources at their institution specific to their interests, while some older ones will have a deeper and longer appreciation for the role of the library in the institution. Necessarily, librarians are looking for ways to overcome the bleak prospects for more funding at a time of increased research. Open access in general, and IRs specifically, are one way to begin to address what for most institutions has been a steady decline in purchase power, with little relief in sight.

Not all will agree that a review of the economic landscape of scholarly communication need or even should be an element of the marketing message. Objections include the fact that this is a negative message, and the message should be kept positive; that the primary functions of the IR complement the work of publishers, not compete with them (and many faculty will be working for the publishers, as editors or reviewers, or will otherwise hold mostly positive opinions about them); and that published content is not the best target content for the IR anyway.

Unquestionably, however, including this background drives home the point that change is already happening, because libraries are less and less able to deliver the information that their users need, and that faculty and others need to acknowledge this and take steps to address it. Even without an IR, the library needs to be delivering this message to the institution. With an IR, library staff move beyond raising awareness of the problem to actively presenting a means of doing something about it. Because addressing the problem of increasingly insufficient budgets is and has been a fundamental reason that libraries are implementing IRs, and because this implementation is often seen as one component in a comprehensive plan to address scholarly communication issues, it is nothing more or less than being honest to share this with the audience. Indeed, because almost all IRs do originate from within the library, it may be that without this economic background forcing the issue, there would be many fewer IRs than there are.

There are of course other reasons for an institution to be running an IR. Storage and preservation of institutional content are important functions, and this is a library role very familiar to faculty and others. Content disappears daily from institutional Web sites, and too often no one is assigned an oversight role for that content. Its management is haphazard or nonexistent, although the same is not true for traditional print equivalents. An IR provides the platform for managing this amorphous mass of information.

What the Benefits Are and Why the Individual Should Contribute

This, of course, is the whole heart of the message. This is also where picking the precise elements for the audience will be essential. To that end, this is where any information gleaned from a survey will be applied, or, more likely, where staff familiarity with the research and output of an institution, department, or individual will reap dividends.

Any given community of researchers or producers of information is going to have some needs that are currently unmet by whatever information dissemination model is in place. Scientists and social scientists cannot include data along with their journal articles and have no easy way to share their data; educators have no ideal unrestricted place to disseminate support materials they have developed for their courses; conference organizers have no access to a submission tool or easy way to organize proceedings. An IR can answer these and other needs, but choosing wisely which to present in a limited time to a busy audience will determine whether that audience comes back for more help.

There are numerous benefits to an IR, and each one can be described in greater or lesser detail, as needed. The three most essential benefits are

- increased access,
- more visibility, and
- better preservation.

Increased Access

As mentioned, without the increasing problem of institutional and especially library budgets insufficient to acquire the resources needed by researchers, it is questionable whether IRs would be as popular projects as they are. This problem is a major driver for IR development, as librarians and others explore new ways to disseminate research and creative efforts of all kinds. Increased access is an essential problem for researchers and scholars and an essential benefit of IRs.

How this translates into a message for an audience may vary, depending on the nature of the position that members hold, promotional process, and any altruistic impulses they might have. Taking the last first, it is not unlikely that there are people within any research institution who believe that they are not doing their research in order for someone else to make a profit off of it. Particularly in education institutions, there will be those who want to share their efforts with as wide an audience as possible, simply for the sake of sharing. In fact, these individuals are more likely to personally initiate contact with IR staff for participation and to serve as pioneers for the institution. It would be unwise to completely omit this aspect of what an IR can do, because not everyone will react positively to direct appeals to their self-interest as the only reason to participate.

While these "do gooders" will be important players, there will be few of them. Other appeals will attract a wider pool of contributors. Those inside of the tough tenure process, in particular, can find some value in participation. An IR can help them make their case for promotion and tenure, because open access has been shown to increase the use of research. Studies have shown that it leads directly to increased citations (Harnad and Brody, 2004; MacCallum and Parthasarathy, 2006). If nothing else, most IRs can and do provide download statistics to authors, not something normally provided by a journal or other publisher. Also, some granting agencies and institutions have it as a goal or requirement that the results of funded research or other efforts be disseminated for the public benefit. Posting materials in an IR can help to satisfy this requirement.

More Visibility

Furthermore, an IR that is compliant with the standard for open access data, specifically OAI-PMH (the Open Archives Initiative Protocol for Metadata Harvesting), increases the chance of discovery for IR contents and provides more visibility. This includes ranking in search engines, including both Google and Google Scholar, as well as other harvesters of IR content, most notably OAISter, which will find content that search engines such as Google do not. This means that by posting content in a repository, authors are expanding the reach of their research beyond what can be achieved by simply putting the content on a departmental or individual Web site—or even by having it published.

> OAISter was developed by the University of Michigan and the University of Illinois. See **www.oaister.org**.

Better Preservation

In addition, an IR provides a measure of preservation far superior to what a departmental or individual Web site can provide. First, an IR should provide permanent URLs to the contents. This means, unlike so many institutional Web pages, the location and URL for the materials will not change. Once established, they are there for good, so they can be distributed to colleagues, and posted on individual Web sites, with peace of mind. Beyond this, IRs need to be backed up regularly. Commercial services will provide this function as part of their standard contract. Locally implemented IRs will need to include this as part of the ordinary IR operation and need to account for this service, as explained in Chapter 2. This backup provides a measure of reliability not necessarily present with other institutional Web sites. Finally, an IR will typically carry a commitment to migrate content, to the extent possible, or at the very least to preserve the data.

These three benefits form the core elements of any message about the IR, and they are applicable to each and every submission. Other elements will be more dependent on the local institution and the needs of its members and also on the platform in use.

Other Benefits

Google Analytics (**www.google.com/analytics**) provides use statistics and is free and easy to use, although the data collected are limited.

One of the most compelling benefits IR staff can offer their contributor pool is the availability of download statistics. This represents a clear indicator of the use of a researcher's efforts, something that journal publishers do not provide. If the platform makes a distinction between abstract or other intermediate views and full-text downloads, authors can get a clear picture of how many people are actually reading or otherwise using their work as opposed to the nebulous information provided by other means, for example, how many libraries have purchased a book or have a journal subscription. Download data have been used in promotion and tenure cases, although it is unknown to what extent and to what effect. Nevertheless, this is an easily understood, tangible benefit that has resonated with content creators. Regular, automatic notification to authors of this data is a decided advantage for a platform.

It is widely recognized that the level of collaboration among researchers of different departments or institutions is higher than ever before. One implication of this is a need for a protected, shared work space, where progress can be reported, data shared, etc. An IR can typically serve this function by providing restricted access to a flexible site that can accommodate multiple file types and different versions of those files. This will appeal to many researchers engaged in interdisciplinary or interinstitutional research projects.

An IR provides a platform for content types not often supported by departmental or other institutional Web sites. By providing a convenient infrastructure, IRs are an attractive choice for presenting these alternative content types, including conference proceedings and presentations, educational support materials, technical reports, and working papers.

For more traditional types of publishing, there are increasingly more supplementary files that are associated with the publication but cannot be accommodated by the traditional journal or book. Such files may include data sets and audio or video files. An IR can accommodate these materials, and keep them associated with the "parent" document by either linking to or including the document itself and applying appropriate metadata.

If the IR software supports journal publishing, this can be a distinct benefit to offer the institution. Bepress' Digital Commons is noteworthy in this regard, as it was originally developed for online journal publication and has the tools necessary to effectively deliver journals. Peer-review tracking is the most important of these. In addition, the underlying structure is such that the appearance of an online journal on a Digital Commons site has the features and layout customary to an online journal that are familiar to its readers. For other platforms, this structure and appearance has to be created from scratch and is a more difficult (though not impossible) proposition.

How to Proceed

The last essential element of any marketing message is how those interested in pursuing participation should proceed. Obviously, contact information needs to be provided. A decision will need to be made by the repository staff about what steps are necessary before a repository presence is established. The most realistic and supportive guidelines will allow creating a space in the IR with no more than an okay from a single member of any particular community; a more conservative approach, which would protect against any complaints or blowback, would require some sort of vetting process by the community as a whole or its administrators, such as a chair or dean. The latter approach will delay progress, but the institutional environment may demand it.

It is also possible with the message to indicate the actual steps required for the initial setup: deciding on a name for the community, any subcommunities, and any series beneath those communities. Any descriptive language and logos need to be identified and shared with the managers. If there are to be separate policies for the series, beyond the standard IR policies, these will need to be created as well. Determining who will do the submissions and who will serve as series administrators is also necessary. Here too, these steps may either be required before setup or be worked out after some commitment to participate has been gained. A rigid set of steps will protect staff from the results of misunderstanding, the most significant of which is likely to be that they assume responsibility for some or all of these decisions or functions; however, adhering to these rigid rules will certainly delay, and potentially discourage, participation.

Delivering the Message

Just as the members of any institution have diverse ways of communicating information, they also have diverse preferences or styles for acquiring information. A marketing plan should reflect this diversity and incorporate a number of ways of delivering the message about the IR.

Rollout

When the IR is being rolled out, a comprehensive marketing plan should be included. The first part of this plan targets the institution's own information-sharing publications. In an academic setting, this would include announcements in the institution's official public relations publication, which almost every institution has; any publication dedicated to highlighting the research of the institution; and the campus newspaper.

Using these publications may present a danger if misinformation is delivered. To the extent possible, it is important for the IR staff to control the message that is communicated in these venues, because the information needs to be accurate, and the IR staff is in the best position to emphasize the benefits that will create the biggest impression among the biggest audience. In fact, the staff should write the copy, if allowed, or at least prepare a fact sheet for the authors or editors of the publications. If not able to write the copy, IR staff should ask to see the text before it is published, to verify facts and to make sure vital information is included. While there may be other articles or columns about the IR down the road, there is only one rollout, and its announcement should be done right.

See **http://opensiuc.lib.siu.edu/morris_opensiuc/1/** for an example of a rollout brochure.

Staff can take control of the message by preparing their own publication or promotional material and distributing it themselves. Depending on the funding available, this should be as visually attractive as possible. However, even a simple one-page text flyer, such as are tacked to bulletin boards all over university campuses, serves a purpose. Even better is a color brochure or pamphlet, designed to capture the eye. It is a good idea to enlist the help of graphic designers in this effort; again, though, it is important for the staff to control the actual message.

Most IRs are run from within the library. While this is desirable, it is also important to have the IR recognized as an institutionwide service and resource. For this reason, it is not necessary, and may be undesirable, for the promotional materials to be prominently stamped with the library's name, logo, or other identifier. These materials represent an ideal opportunity to have the IR identified with the entire institution, not just with the library or whatever department or office has administrative responsibility.

In the same vein, space permitting, supportive comments from a well-recognized—and well-liked—member of the institution are a good addition. The appropriate comments, taking into account the space available, the audience, etc., can be prepared for approval from the supporter so that a simple acquiescence is all that is required on his or her part. As will be discussed in the next chapter, this identification of an institutional advocate, outside of the IR staff, can go a long way to spreading the word and the appeal of the IR, and it is a primary tactic for achieving institutional buy-in.

The e-mail address should use the name of the repository, e.g., **OpenSIUC@lib.siu.edu**.

The promotional materials, as well as the announcements, should also clearly indicate the name of the repository and provide contact information, including e-mail addresses and phone numbers. If the repository is administered by a team, it is advisable to create a unified e-mail address so that any e-mail sent to that address is then distributed to all members of the team. This way, there is a guarantee that someone will respond to any contacts made by e-mail.

This raises an issue of common complaint about IRs—that, too often, no contact information for the individuals actually responsible for management of the IR is presented on the IR site itself. At best, a generic e-mail link is provided. This is bad management. Some will be put off by the unavailability of an actual person to contact. Names, e-mail addresses, and phone numbers provide a more personalized touch to what can be an impersonal service. Fear of being overwhelmed by contacts generated from listing this information is completely unfounded and unwarranted.

In general, this same information should be provided on all marketing materials. The sole exception would be for those materials that are costly to produce and are intended to last or be distributed over an extended period of time, as coordinators and other IR staff may come and go. Here, general contact information should be provided instead, such as the distributed e-mail address or a general library phone number.

These types of communication may not result in immediate responses from the community, but they lay the ground for further communication and play an essential role in the overall marketing plan for the IR.

After Rollout

Except for unusual cases, growth of the repository will at first be slow. It may have a skeleton appearance in these early days. For this reason, some of the techniques described in this section may be better implemented later on, once the repository has put some meat on its bones.

Just as avoiding the library stamp, and using the institution's identifiers instead, may be wise, having links to the IR from the institution's Web site will help to give it recognition and standing beyond that of the library. It should certainly be included in any section of the institution's Web site dealing with research. Other potential areas where links might be included are sections designated for faculty and any alphabetical index or site map. Obviously, as a library service—or even if it is not—it should be linked to from the library's site, also in multiple places. Getting it on the front page may be a difficult battle to win, given the fight for that prime real estate, but it is a battle worth fighting. The fact that a repository is a service, a resource, and possibly a department or unit, and thus does not fit into any of the typical Web site divisions, may help make the case. Links from multiple places within the library's Web site are appropriate—in sections for services, collections, research, faculty tools, are all possible.

An open meeting to announce, describe, and push the repository can be used to generate more publicity. First, the publicity announcing the meeting—using the same venues as the announcement of the repository itself—provides another exposure opportunity. The meeting itself can use prominent speakers—from either within or outside the institution—to help raise the profile and stature of the IR. Speakers do not have to be experts on IRs. A theme can be established around an issue raised by speakers, and then the IR can be presented as a solution. So, a meeting on open access, featuring speakers with some role in the movement, can start off with discussion of new forms of communication of research and end with the description of the institution's own new channel, the IR.

Just as identifying internal advocates is crucial for establishing some content base to build on, these same advocates can help with such a presentation. They provide an element of authority difficult to match by library staff. They can talk about personal, real-life experiences in preparing and disseminating research that will be similar to others' experiences.

On a smaller scale, a similar presentation to the repository staff's own colleagues should be held at this stage, because it is important to have buy-in from them as much as from the contributor pool. This is especially true in the academic library setting, where these colleagues—especially subject librarians or liaisons—may need to be active participants and advocates for the IR. They will need to be well-versed in the role and value of IRs and to be able to talk intelligently about them in a variety of settings.

To this end, support materials for less experienced or less knowledgeable colleagues are advisable if they are to have any part in the marketing, development, and expansion of the IR. The types and amounts of these materials should reflect different levels of comfort and different levels of interaction, from a simple cheat sheet to a full presentation. A set of talking points, which frames a complete discussion of the IR but which can be cherry-picked from by a knowledgeable colleague appropriate to the audience, is the minimum resource required. Mastering these elements also provides the framework for an "elevator talk," i.e., an opportunity that arises by chance to talk with a potential contributor and in five minutes or less get the message across. Talking points should discuss the following:

See, for example, **http://opensiuc.lib.siu.edu/morris_opensiuc/2**.

- What an IR is
- What the benefits are
- How it is organized and administered
- What can go in
- Who can contribute
- What the submission process is
- What the next steps are

Repository staff can also provide a list of commonly asked questions. While to some extent this may be institution specific, or even community specific, there are some questions that seem to be universally asked:

- If I already have documents on my personal or departmental Web site, why would I want to put them in the repository?
- Doesn't copyright prevent using the IR for posting of published materials?
- Does posting in a repository constitute prior publication? That is, will publishers reject my submission because it's already been distributed in this way?
- What about works produced by multiple contributors at multiple institutions?
- What happens if I leave the institution?

- Can access be restricted? Embargoed?
- Can materials be withdrawn?

Some of those responsible for outreach may want even more of a safety net, so a full presentation, using presentation software, can also be developed. Such a presentation allows the message to be taken on the road, any place, any time. The presentation should at a minimum incorporate the talking points. Much more can go into the presentation, which can then be pared down as desired. Screenshots should be included in case there is no Internet connection available at the presentation site.

Preparing these training resources represents a significant time commitment up front, but, once done, they should not require a great deal of further attention. The repository itself can be used to disseminate them, as many repositories include a series for documents related to the IR.

Hard Work

Regardless of the techniques used, gathering content can be slow work. The IR is essentially an innovation, and most content creators need time to adjust to innovations. Inertia is strong, even in institutions with the brightest and most creative minds. In academia, any threat to traditional publication processes—particularly journals—may be seen as threatening and will almost certainly tread on some (editor or reviewer) toes. Also, most IR benefits are not immediate, though they are by no means entirely abstract. Participation also requires some time and effort on somebody's part, which is often in scarce supply.

For these reasons, there will be reluctance or even resistance to participation. No amount of clever marketing techniques will overcome this entirely. What can overcome these obstacles is hard work. Meeting with individuals, assessing their needs, talking up the repository and demonstrating how it can address those needs, stressing the benefits of most relevance to different audiences—young and old, scientist and artist, faculty and student, all will help to gain contributors and supporters. Phone calls, office visits, serendipitous discussions—these are all part of a marketing operation too. Indeed, they are the most enduring and effective marketing activities and can never really be said to end. This is because gathering content and expanding the IR—the subject of the next chapter—can never be said to end, either.

References

Harnad, Stevan and Tim Brody. 2004. "Comparing the Impact of Open Access (OA) vs. Non-OA Articles in the Same Journals." *D-Lib Magazine* 10, no. 6. Available: www.dlib.org/dlib/june04/harnad/06harnad.html (accessed October 15, 2008).

Jenkins, Barbara, Elizabeth Breakstone, and Carol Hixson. 2005. "Content In, Content Out: The Dual Roles of the Reference Librarian in Institutional Repositories." *Reference Services Review* 33, no. 3: 312–324.

Lynch, Clifford. 2003. "Institutional Repositories: Essential Infrastructure for Scholarship in the Digital Age." *ARL Bimonthly Report* no. 226 (February). Available: www.arl.org/resources/pubs/br/br226/br226ir.shtml (accessed October 21, 2008).

MacCallum. C.J. and Parthasarathy, H. 2006. "Open Access Increases Citation Rate." *PLoS Biology* 4, no. 5: e176. Available: http://dx.doi.orgdoi:10.1371/journal.pbio.0040176 (accessed October 21, 2008).

Collection Development and Expansion

6

IN THIS CHAPTER:

While it is true that there is no substitute for hard work in growing an institutional repository (IR), there are some tried and true methods that have helped IR staffs worldwide increase the content in their institutional repositories. Using these techniques will begin to lay the groundwork for further growth and success. They can be initiated before the repository is even live, because, while planning an IR involves significant time upfront, some of this planning effort will require waiting, such as for meetings with, or answers from, vendors, administrative review of an initial proposal, etc. This downtime can be used to begin to explore the content recruitment efforts described in this chapter. In fact, as will become clear, when maintaining an IR, there is no such thing as downtime. There is always some content to be identified, some new author to be approached. Identifying and gathering this content, even before the IR is implemented, is a strong first step to success.

Gathering Low-Hanging Fruit

An empty repository does not make an attractive selling point. It is important to have some content right from the start, to aid in further recruitment efforts. This way, when meeting with potential contributors, it can be demonstrated that there has already been some buy-in from the institution and individual members. The impediment of being the first to try something new is thus removed. Also, showing the layout and appearance of the IR—a sample community and series—makes it easier to convey how the site is structured and what someone's presence or contribution will look like. A picture is worth a thousand words, and some visible structure will aid in recruitment efforts.

This is why "low-hanging fruit" should be the first target of any new repository. What is low-hanging fruit? First, it is the content that is already available on the institution's various Web pages. Generally, the only issue that will arise in gathering this content is addressing why the author should bother putting it in the IR. After all, it is already available to the outside world, so accessibility is not an issue. Still, if additional persuasion is needed, the major benefits identified in the previous chapter apply to this content too: the IR will make it more visible and will provide a stronger preservation commitment.

Second, there have often been feelers put out over the years by various communities within the institution toward the library, asking what the library can do to help make accessible and preserve some existing material. Those making the requests may not have known it, but what they are asking for is a repository; it is simply a matter then of informing them about the service, explaining how it meets their needs, and getting a commitment from them to participate. Library administrators and subject liaisons may be aware of these requests, and they should be sought out for this information. Subject liaisons, too, should have an awareness of what content already exists on department sites, so they have an important role to play even at this beginning stage. This is why it is important to involve them in the project from its initiation.

One of the advantages of targeting low-hanging fruit from the start is that, most likely, it will provide an opportunity to get content from a variety of communities, in a variety of formats, for a variety of purposes. In the academic setting, there will be some authors who will have posted their published articles on their individual Web sites—legally or not. Similarly, there will likely be some conference papers or presentations, working papers, and technical reports already on Web sites. There may be some journals, open access titles run by faculty, as well as student-run titles, that can be added. Depending on the guidelines established for the repository, another source of content is the institutional newsletters and archival records that should be available at almost every institution.

Concentrating early efforts on gathering this content can provide a well-balanced collection, some part of which will appeal to someone else in the institution. It is the easiest way to gather the most content possible in a short period of time. It also lays the groundwork for more outreach efforts, leads to discussions with the contributor pool, and begins to generate download statistics that help justify the expenditure for an IR and proves its viability.

Catching the Big Fish

As mentioned in Chapter 5, it can be extremely useful to attract the support of some internal advocates, particularly individuals with strong pull within the institution—not necessarily administrative pull, but intellectual or personal pull, natural leaders who others will listen to when they speak and follow where they lead (Jenkins, Breakstone, and Hixson, 2005). Academic institutions are notoriously composed of independent-minded individuals, but, for historical reasons, internal politics, or self-interest, some successful individuals will have achieved some level of high status on campus. Getting their support and participation is an incomparable success.

There are two ways to go about this. One is to identify these individuals and then approach them about lending their support, convincing them that they should lend their name and time to the effort. Essentially, this is not seeking out natural advocates but, instead, making them. This is sound, but it may involve more time and effort—and result in more failure—than the alternative, which is to identify those who are already involved in alternative methods of information dissemination and who thus may be readily inclined to give their support.

One place to start is to look for editors of open access journals and authors who regularly contribute to them. Their commitment to alternatives has in this way already been demonstrated, although it is not always easy to know what their motivations are for participation in open access efforts. Some may support open access journals but not be supportive of IRs. Nevertheless, they are a logical first target and a potential boon to a beginning IR (Palmer, Teffeau, and Newton, 2008).

Another place to start is to identify the institution's high-profile individuals and then examine their Web sites—assuming they have one—to see if they have already posted some of their documents there. If so, they may be easy to persuade to help, because they have already taken the time and trouble to try to disseminate their research this way. Doing so is a clear demonstration that the individual is aware of the limitations of the standard methods of communication and is trying to do something about it. Any study of an academic Web site will show that some authors are making this attempt, but many are not.

It is not only authors and editors who should be targeted in their role as leaders in the institution. Administrators too can provide a significant push for the IR with their vocal support or leading by example. Their contributions do not begin and end with the marketing efforts described in the previous chapter. As researchers themselves, any participation from them may serve as a spark for others in their discipline. Administratively, they are in a position to push the IR as a priority to their staffs and colleagues. Indeed, some of the more successful efforts have resulted from getting buy-in from an administrator who then, either by official mandate or not, is able to force the issue and get participation rates that would otherwise be difficult to achieve (see, for example, Cohen and Schmidle, 2007). Support at this level is a real plus and worth additional effort. The recruitment function of the IR may serve as a compelling feature for administrators, at multiple levels, and help to gain their support.

Copyright Issues

Copyright issues are the major hurdle facing IR staff. This is particularly true for journal articles, the predominant means of communication in the sciences, holding nearly that position in the social sciences and a lesser, though by no means marginal, role in the arts and humanities. For material that has been, or is intended to be, published elsewhere, copyright has to be accounted for. This should not cause panic, however, as following a few simple guidelines will help to ensure compliance without overly restricting or discouraging contributions.

Copyright Basics, available online from the U.S. Copyright Office at **www.copyright.gov/circs/circ1.pdf**, provides essential information for all those involved in information dissemination, including IR staff.

For copyrighted material, it is necessary to identify what rights have been retained by the author. This content is often the hardest to get into the repository and is also the most attractive, because it is often the most sought after and the most downloaded. It is not as problematic as it may seem at first, but it is the hardest to get in a format that is legal to post in the repository. This is because most publishers do not allow the posting of their final, edited and formatted version of the author's manuscript into IRs. At the time of submission, authors are typically required to assign all, or most, publication and distribution rights to the publisher. When they do so, they sign away the right to distribute their own research in such manner as they see fit—including via IRs. Some publishers do allow authors to retain some distribution rights, under certain circumstances.

If the right to post the publisher's version on a personal or institutional Web site is not retained, authors and IR staff are left with the version originally sent to the publisher (the preprint) or with the final edited version, revised after the peer review or other editing process (the postprint). Often, neither version is still available to the author. This may be because it has been discarded or lost, a coauthor at another institution is the only one to have it, or it is in an unusable format. Whatever the case, this has proven to be the major stumbling block to populating IRs. Even when such versions are available, they are more difficult to find, request, and acquire than are the publisher's final version, which may be readily accessible to the IR staff or author. This is a significant source of frustration to IR staff, and there is no magic bullet to solve this problem.

This is because it is incumbent on IR staff to adhere to publisher policies on self-archiving, including the posting of a document in an IR. While many authors, especially faculty, regularly post publisher versions of their own articles on their individual Web sites, they do so contrary to the terms of their signed agreements with publishers. They are not pursued, primarily because it is beyond the capabilities of most publishers to systematically track all the authors who publish in their journals. This may especially be the case for those publishers with thousands of journals in their portfolio. However, it would be much easier for these same publishers to go to a single site where all of an institution's publications—often identified as something like "faculty publications" or "peer-reviewed research"—are located in one place. This, after all, is one of the functions of the IR—to group all of that content into one place. Any one institution may be targeted as a test case, similar to the way Georgia State was targeted by publishers for its electronic reserves practices (Albanese, 2008). Furthermore, systematic abuse of author/publisher agreements is certain to backfire, potentially entailing the imposition of more restrictive archiving and posting policies.

It is therefore necessary to identify publisher policies before processing copyrighted content. The first place to look for what rights an author retains to his work is in the author agreement that every publisher requires upon manuscript submission. Usually, it will be spelled out what the author can and cannot do with the article. The information in this agreement will override any other source of information. Most authors, however, will not have kept this information and will be largely ignorant of the terms of the agreement. Signing one is just an automatic response. Indeed, one of the functions of an IR outreach effort is to educate authors about typical agreement terms and advocate for the retention of more rights by the author, for the author. Because these publisher agreements are almost always unavailable, uncovering the author's rights involves more work. Fortunately, a recent development has helped lessen this work.

Sherpa/RoMEO

Publisher policies on distribution are diverse, and tracking them down can still be a problem. However, as a response to this arduous work, an effort has been underway since 2003 to compile all of this information and make it available to IR managers and others interested in determining what can be done with published journal articles. This site is RoMEO, maintained by Sherpa, a consortium of universities in the United Kingdom. RoMEO (Rights MEtadata for Open archiving) provides, by publisher, information on the default policies regarding the posting of preprints and postprints, the conditions for such postings, and links to the publisher policy Web page, when available. In addition, each publisher is assigned a color code:

> For more information on RoMEO, visit **www.sherpa.ac.uk/romeo**.

Green for those who allow posting of preprints and postprints

Blue for those who allow posting of postprints (which may or may not include the publisher's version)

Yellow for those who allow posting of preprints

White for those who do not allow posting of any version

RoMEO also provides information on when the information was last updated and a way to suggest updating for each publisher, as well as a way to request that Sherpa seek information for a given publisher. It has become the default source of information on publisher policies for IR staff around the world, and it serves as a reliable one-stop clearinghouse, which significantly reduces the time required for getting this content into a repository. Because the information provided in RoMEO is taken directly from the publisher, with direct communication between Sherpa and publisher when needed, repository staff can be comfortable in following the guidelines provided there. The site is continually growing, but not all publishers are listed there.

Beyond RoMEO

For those publications that are not listed in RoMEO, and otherwise lacking an author agreement, it is necessary to contact the publisher directly. This will certainly add delay to the process. As IR staffs around the world pursue this information, publishers are forced to think about the issue and, hopefully, develop a policy. IR staff who do initiate such requests for information from a publisher should consider also recommending that the publisher submit the information to Sherpa. This will help to reduce redundant efforts.

A similar process is necessary for other types of published material, including book chapters, book reviews, and abstracts. For these, Sherpa is not an adequate source, for it deals strictly with articles. Publishers will have different policies for different types of publications, and as yet there is no site similar to Sherpa for information for other publications. The author agreement, if available, or direct communication with the publisher is required.

It has been possible in some cases to retroactively acquire the rights to published articles. Some libraries have, as a part of subscription negotiations, successfully bargained for the right to deposit published articles by the institution's authors from previous years. This can result in sizable additions to the IR in a short period of time. These negotiations have not always proved successful, but the reward makes the attempt worthwhile and the worst that can happen is the publisher refuses.

Discussion of all of this with authors, of course, becomes a teachable moment, as librarians can and should be explaining the implications of the signing away of rights at the time of submission of an article or other intellectual work. Many author addendums available now can be used to request self-archiving rights—including the posting in a repository—from the publisher (Hirtle, 2006). Authors should be alerted to them and be encouraged to use them.

See **http://oad.simmons.edu/oadwiki/Author_addenda** for a list of addendums.

One last word about copyright. A copyright violation is probably the most likely reason for the withdrawal of IR content. There is no track record and no reason to believe that an incidental violation of copyright will lead to punitive legal action, provided any publisher's request to remove the offending content from the repository is followed. Repository staff should exercise due diligence in determining the status of a particular document, just as library staff have always done when dealing with reserves, interlibrary loan, etc. In some cases, despite all efforts to determine a document's intellectual property disposition, a subjective call must be made. In these cases, fear should not be the overriding guide.

Letting Go of Preconceptions: Content and Content Providers

It is not unusual for new repositories to have firm guidelines for content, reflecting firm ideas of IR managers about what the IR should be. It is also not unusual for IRs to be sorely underpopulated. It may take a while, but even the firmest managers may come around to the idea that they may have to expand the IR's horizons if any level of success is to be achieved.

If published research is the goal, and efforts to gather it prove unavailing, other types of material will need to be targeted. Gray literature, student output, and archival records are the most likely targets. Many might protest that gathering these types of content does nothing to address the fundamental problems in the dissemination of scholarly research, one of the purported reasons for starting and maintaining IRs. The point is valid but does not address the facts that publisher policies may block inclusion, authors may be unwilling to submit manuscript versions that do not have the authority and attraction of publisher formatting, or acquiring such publications has a modest track record of success, at best. Barring institutional mandates (discussed later), government regulation, or organized opposition from researchers the world over, the problems of gathering published research in repositories will continue to frustrate efforts solely or even predominantly targeting these materials.

However, there is a wealth of other material to be gathered. Indeed, many of these types of content will benefit from IR exposure more than published research, which does at least have some guaranteed circulation, dwindling though it may be. But working papers, conference presentations, technical reports, data sets—all of these may have little or no exposure at all. Demonstrated demand for this content, as measured by downloads, is incontrovertible, often to the surprise of authors and IR managers alike. One of the attractions of IRs is that they often defy conventional wisdom and reveal unpredictable information needs.

> According to *Merriam-Webster Online* (**www.merriam-webster.com/dictionary/gray+literature**), gray literature is "written material (as a report) that is not published commercially or is not generally accessible."

Archival Records and Publications

Archival records have not demonstrated this unrecognized attraction, but they do serve a more purely institutional purpose. While certainly less sexy than high download numbers that may come with higher profile works, meeting the local need to store and save records can attract ongoing institutional support. In fact, it may even aid in efforts to procure funding beyond the library, where IR funding typically comes from. This is because these materials have relevance to administrators more immediately than does the research or creative output of the institution's employees. Records may include meeting minutes, official policies, internal and external review documents, etc. Undergoing accreditation reviews, tracking institutional policies and their versions, and documenting governance functions can all benefit from the use of the repository. It may be easiest to identify the needs in this area with representation on governance bodies, such as academic committees. Scanning administration Web sites may also provide some leads.

In addition to these records, institutional publications such as newsletters may also be targeted for inclusion. There may be publications at different levels of the institution, from the university to the college or school to the department, so that a great deal of content may be readily available.

The primary benefit of using the IR for these types of documents is certainly archival. Stability and backup are essential for these materials, and the IR should be presented as the single best local service to provide these two functions.

Conferences

Almost every academic institution will host a variety of conferences, seminar or lecture series, or other gatherings. The output of these events will vary, but, to the extent that there is output, IR staff should seek to include it in the IR. Otherwise, the content is ephemeral, and exposure is limited to those who happen to be available for the event. In times of decreasing funding for all activities, including travel, it may be easier to convince organizers of the need for, and benefit of, recording and preserving the content from their events and making it available to a wider audience. Conferences provide the opportunity to include content in diverse formats: papers that are presented, presentation shows that are used to support them, and audio and video files for those that are digitally recorded.

It is important to initiate discussions with organizers before the event, for a couple of reasons. First, the event may be the only reason a particular group or series of speakers or presenters are together, and they will be scattered after the event, so seeking their cooperation in providing their content or acquiring their permission to post it in the repository will be more difficult. More complete coverage of the event will be possible with earlier discussions. Second, providing space in the repository for organizers may allow them to use the submission process as part of any review activity associated with the event, which may help efforts to encourage them to use the repository. When possible, this allows the repository to actually support the event's organization, rather than merely disseminate the results.

Data Sets

Data sets come in a wide variety of formats and types. They may be merely a jumble of numbers in a text file or on a Web page, or they may be in a file format associated with a specific application, such as Excel or SPSS. They may include formatting structure or be in a simple list. Whatever the case, data sets are a viable option for any IR. In fact, because there is no copyrighting of data (at least in the United States), they may be an easy target for repository growth.

Many times, there is no other presentation venue for the data collected by researchers. It may be presented in an abbreviated way in a formal publication, but that does not represent the full use or value of the data. Making it available for other researchers expands its usefulness, and many researchers are searching for ways to expand its availability.

Data sets do present some unique challenges for IR staff. To make it useful, descriptive metadata and/or text beyond what is normally required for documents are necessary. This is because the only searchable part of the data are numbers—and, because no one will be using a search engine to search specific numbers, discovery of the data sets will be impossible without some information about the data—what it describes, how it was collected, and how it can be used. It is important, much more so than for a journal article or any other full-text searchable file, to have the authors themselves provide this descriptive information. Information can be added as additional metadata fields. Some institutions include a separate, associated file that describes multiple aspects of the data. Because this file is then discoverable by search engines, access to the data set is enhanced. The other significant challenge is the sheer size of some data sets. Regardless of the repository platform, any commitment to accommodate researchers' data will have to be limited by size restrictions.

Note that inclusion of data sets is not the equivalent of data curation, although it shares some of the same functions and goals. Data curation often involves institutional data generated by the operations of that institution—for an academic institution, student data such as financial aid, grades, etc., as well as enrollment figures, grant receipts, etc. A fuller description of data curation is beyond the scope of this book, but it is important not to be so overwhelmed by the challenge that inclusion of data sets is avoided.

Education Support Materials

Research is usually seen as the primary target of a repository. Academic institutions, however, produce a considerable amount of material that is designed to support these institutions' other role: education. Faculty routinely create materials for the classroom. These materials are used to supplement textbooks, journal articles, and other published materials that make up the required and suggested reading for the class. Often, these locally created files are stored behind a course management system, reaching only a small audience, and are then removed at the end of each semester. Even on the Web page of a faculty member, they have little stability and no guarantee of being around for any length of time. Some IR staff, therefore, have targeted this material as well as the research output of the institution.

This material can be harder to identify and collect, because it is created for, and disseminated to, a particular class. It may not be readily discoverable by scanning Web sites. Faculty may never have considered it worthy of preservation and extended dissemination, and so they may need to be convinced that there is a (free) market for this content, too. Gathering this content thus requires individual meetings to determine what is out there and to make the case for including it in the repository. The benefits of not having to remove and reload it, move it to a new Web site, or manage it at all beyond updating or adding to it will help make the case. Some faculty, and some institutions, are focused more on education than research; these individuals should be known to subject liaisons and identifiable as those having received teaching awards or other similar recognition. They comprise the first target of early adopters for this category of content.

Student Publications

It is not necessary or even advisable to seek to include all student publications. As discussed in Chapter 4, some are simply not of adequate quality to provide the desirable impression on outsiders. Without getting involved in the time-consuming task of document-by-document review, IR staff can set guidelines for inclusion that will help to weed out most of the least worthy submissions.

One simple way to do this is to allow submissions only from graduate students. While not all graduate work is of high quality, it is generally better than that of undergraduates and also has the benefit of showing to prospective graduate students what they might expect from their experience at the institution and what is expected of them to succeed.

Some content of this type will cross over with other types; for example, conference presentations and even journal publications. Graduate students in particular do produce both. In most cases, it will be most advantageous, for the growth of the repository, to separate student submissions from faculty submissions. The latter will not be particularly impressed with the idea of including their production in the same space as that of students, even of their own students. For some, it will even be a sufficient reason not to participate. Therefore, communities or series designated for students should be created and kept separate from faculty contributions. Whether this is done within the established structure (a series for student publications within an academic department, for example) or with a new structure (a top-level community for students with subcommunities for academic departments, for example) does not make much difference as long as the distinction is clear.

There is some work from undergraduate students that may be deemed appropriate for the repository. Most institutions will have an honors program or other program that allows students preferential research opportunities and requires a presentation or paper at the end of the experience. These end products are common IR targets, again because they serve as recruitment tools and typically are of better quality than the average undergraduate work. Undergraduate journal publications, such as collections of fiction or poetry, may also be included in the repository, whether the justification be for accessibility or, more likely, preservation.

Electronic Theses and Dissertations

Theses and dissertations have been one of the raisons d'être for IRs. They possess many of the attributes that make them a natural for this method of dissemination: copyright is retained by the author; in most cases these days they are born digital; authors are actively seeking recognition in their fields and are often happy to have an easy opportunity to be included; and the works truly are the products of a specific institution, as a consequence of its academic departments, research focus, and faculty advisors. All of these factors make them an attractive target for early ingestion into the repository (Fyffe and Welburn, 2008).

Most advanced degree-granting institutions have agreements with ProQuest for the storing, preservation, and dissemination of their PhD dissertations. A smaller number also submit master's theses to ProQuest for the same purposes. It is a mistake, however, to assume that this constitutes a sufficient level of involvement, if information dissemination, program marketing, and student support are deemed essential functions of the institution. This is because ProQuest is a commercial service, which demands payment for its services, thereby restricting access and distribution of locally produced materials. Essentially, authors—in this case graduate students—through long hours and persistent efforts, create a research document and then grant distribution and commercial rights to that document to a company after delivering the said document to the company in the format and manner of its choosing. This is not to say that ProQuest does not perform a valuable service, for it does, in archiving and preserving the dissertations for hundreds of institutions. Nevertheless, this model, created decades ago, before the advent of the Internet, does not use current technology to maximize information distribution—to the detriment of all, reader, researcher, author, and institution.

This is why so many institutions have begun programs of maintaining their own collections of ETDs (electronic theses and dissertations). Many early adopters created their own systems for storing and sharing ETDs, which was admirable and impressive. Now, however, institutions that are implementing IRs have a better, simpler option and do not need to implement a separate service. In most cases, the distinct functions and characteristics of ETD collections—and there are some aspects that make them distinct from other IR collections—can be accommodated by the major IR software platforms.

The Networked Digital Library of Theses and Dissertations (**www.ndltd.org**) provides support for developing ETDs.

For institutions that are members of ProQuest's program, any concern about the right to post in a repository is unwarranted. At the time of submission of a dissertation or thesis to ProQuest, the author is required to assign only a nonexclusive right to disseminate the document. No permission from ProQuest is required for posting in a repository. However, as is the case with so many journal publishers, there is a restriction against the posting of ProQuest's copyedited version of the document. This means that a separate submission must be made to the IR.

Although inconvenient, this is not insurmountable. Many individuals at many institutions have explored the possibility of simultaneous submission to both ProQuest and the IR, but to no avail so far. However, some institutions have made it possible for the author to do a single submission, either by receiving from ProQuest a copy of the document after the author's submission or by using an original submission to the IR, whose staff or designees then take the additional step of submitting to ProQuest. The latter is the current process in the OhioLink libraries, for example. If an institution has the resources to take this step, it will certainly lead to a higher participation rate. If not, it should still be possible to achieve an acceptable rate of student submissions, because the benefits are clear.

Distributing download statistics to the author is an added benefit that can help to raise participation rates. Including a metadata field for the advisor(s) and/or committee members may help to convince faculty to apply some pressure on their students to participate, as faculty can then easily show to the world a record of the students they have advised. Listing documents not just as part of one large overarching series of ETDs but also including each in a separate series for each department can also be a selling point.

Allowing an embargo period—a set time during which the thesis or dissertation is hidden and only the metadata is shown—can also help raise participation rates. Some students will have concerns that posting in the IR will constitute prior publication, at least for some publishers, and thus diminish their chances of publication. Indeed, this is the policy of some publishers. By instituting an embargo period, the document can be restricted long enough to allow for an attempt to publish the dissertation. If possible, different time periods should be offered; six months, one year, or two years are customary embargo periods. Restricting access to the local institution is usually sufficient to address concerns of prior publication—after all, most institutions have always made a print copy of the dissertation or thesis available to anyone who comes into the library—but it is always best to check with an individual publisher to determine its policy. Regardless of the availability or period of embargoes, it will be necessary to provide an opt out for authors, as some dissertations may contain information related to patentable innovations.

Digitizing

If the library or another department within the institution has a digitization program, either for preservation or access issues for its own collections or to support the digitization of departmental or faculty works, this can be a way to grow the IR. Along with all of the other benefits associated with participation, the digitization itself will be an attractive selling point to faculty and administrators.

There may be opportunities beyond the library to procure funding or other support for these activities. Many library consortia are supporting digitization efforts financially and/or by providing the necessary infrastructure. Collaborating with faculty or others to create project proposals serves as a way not only to generate new IR content but also to establish relationships with potential contributors who may more closely consider the IR for distribution of their other, already digital, content.

Do It Yourself

Ideally, IR management would follow a decentralized model, with individuals in the various departments assuming management and submission responsibilities for their space in the IR. For most institutions, with a limited ability to assign dedicated staff time, this would overcome staffing issues. Realistically, this is very difficult to achieve, because, in order to reach this stage, the department or other unit has to be convinced, as a unit, that the IR is a priority and requires a staffing commitment on their part. Then, some individual can be designated to assume IR duties, receive training, and begin building the collection. This is nice in theory but rare in practice.

Instead, typically IRs have been and continue to be the province of library staff. This may simply reflect that IRs have not reached maturity, and institutions have not yet made the commitment to them—they are still a library-driven project. Until some critical mass is achieved, work will thus continue to fall onto the shoulders of the IR staff. Ironically, the only way out of this scenario may be to expand the workload of IR staff to do some of the grunt work. This means, especially, doing actual submissions. If success breeds success, and this is an equation IR staff have to believe in, then by doing submissions now, the groundwork is being laid for future commitments from other departments and from the institution as a whole. This can be described as the essential gamble of IR staff—without this, nothing good is likely to come of whatever other efforts have been made to establish an IR.

This is why it can be worth the additional expense of hiring a student to do some of the work. Training on how to submit can be done in an hour or less, so there is no great commitment there. With proper oversight, primarily to ensure copyright adherence, content can be added while the IR staff is free to focus on larger issues. The early stage, when the low-hanging fruit is being gathered, is a particularly appropriate time for using student labor.

Integrating the IR into Workflow

Mature IRs will have achieved more than the decentralized management structure described. They will have reached a state where the entire workflow process will be an established part of the routine function of departments and staff involved in the operation. Too often, an IR's success or failure is viewed as the result and responsibility of the extraordinary efforts of a small number of volunteers who have full-time responsibilities elsewhere. To avoid this unfair and potentially self-defeating outlook, collection development processes in particular must be regularized. The two areas with specific relevant responsibilities are *selection* and *processing*.

In academic libraries, selection of materials is most often the domain of the liaisons or, more rarely, bibliographers. Traditionally, selection has predominantly been of resources produced beyond the walls of the campus and published by recognizable publishing companies or other organizations. IRs take selection to another level by targeting everything produced *within* the institution. Even with this goal, however, some selection must be made, driven by the same traditional factors: not everything can be acquired, and not everything should be. Selectors can apply many of the same criteria to the identification of material appropriate to the IR as they have done for other resources. These will include scholarly value, availability, uniqueness, value to the institution and to the community, preservation need, etc. These criteria will be filtered through the goals established for the IR, however. If one goal is to collect student publications, for example, then scholarly value may be deemphasized for that particular collection.

Rather than leaving this important function to an overburdened IR staff, who may simply be trying to gather everything and anything they can, selectors prioritize what to collect and function as criteria by which IR staff develop and implement appropriate marketing activities. Indeed, with reduced purchasing power for nearly all institutions, selection of IR content can serve to replace the increasingly less demanding responsibility for collecting traditional resources. The combination of selection and acquisition of content, via outreach activities, creates a crucial role for liaisons. This is why they are recognized in this book and elsewhere as essential players in IR development and management.

Technical services staff can also play an important role. Adjusting their workflow to include IR-related activities will also contribute to the collection, expansion, and use of content, and it represents a further step in the maturation of the IR. Such activities as metadata creation and cataloging of IR materials (see Chapter 7), creating batch upload files, and maintaining and updating preservation guidelines all contribute to these goals (see, for example, Reese, 2009).

Integrating IR work into the workflow of staff beyond the IR staff represents an institutional commitment to the IR and gets back to the importance of grasping the need for institution in "institutional repository" (see Chapter 2). Ultimately, those institutions that have regularized IR activities in the workflow of their staff will achieve a more consistent and higher level of development than those that do not. Because, as is emphasized throughout this book, the crucial component of IR development is content recruitment, regularizing the workflow for selection activities by liaisons and processing activities for technical services staff is a sound strategy for all IRs and a goal to strive for.

Mandates

No strategy or combination of strategies could achieve the level of success that would follow the implementation of an institutional mandate requiring the depositing of research output into the IR. Such mandates have been successfully implemented at only a handful of institutions or communities within an institution. An examination of the strategies used for accomplishing this notable feat indicates that it has to come from the faculty themselves and not be a library initiative. Mandates have been implemented only where some faculty member or administrator had a longstanding, sincere, and deep commitment to alternative forms of communication, including open access. Nevertheless, it is possible to assist efforts to implement such mandates locally. There are two ways to provide such assistance: make available the method of providing open access, namely, the IR; and prepare the background information that most faculty or other authors will not be familiar with.

In order to do so, IR staff must be prepared to explain and discuss all of the issues surrounding open access and IRs. Typically, this means addressing the fundamental questions about participating, as well as what in Chapter 4 were designated as the policies for a local IR:

- What are the benefits, and why would I want to participate?
- What can be contributed, and how can content be used and by whom?
- What rights are assigned or retained, and why does this need to be done?
- How are submissions to be made and by whom?
- Can materials be withdrawn?
- What file formats are accepted?
- What is the commitment to preservation?
- What does the legal department say about this?

A mandate offers unprecedented ability to expand the IR. No single action can accomplish more, and any opportunity to advance this goal should be taken. Therefore, when looking for "the big fish," the high-profile member of the institution who can lead by example in participating in the repository, this larger goal should be kept in mind. These individuals, if willing, may be able not only to generate interest among their colleagues for participation but also to initiate efforts to implement a local mandate.

New mandates are often announced in Peter Suber's *SPARC Open Access Newsletter* (to subscribe, go to **www.arl.org/sparc/publications/soan**) and are logged at Registry of Open Access Repository Material Archiving Policies (or ROARMAP; (**www.eprints.org/openaccess/policysignup**). Institutions that have recently enacted mandates include the Oregon State University Libraries (**http://ir.library.oregonstate.edu/jspui/bitstream/1957/10850/1/LFA%20Open%20Access%20Mandate.pdf**) and the University of Oregon libraries (**https://mx2.arl.org/Lists/SPARC-OAForum/Message/4943.html**).

Note that a mandate will require additional work with legal counsel, as the institution will be asking for more than voluntary compliance when publisher copyright policies permit. Mandates by their nature require an upfront granting of some distribution rights to the institution by the members or employees for any and all work done by those individuals. This is obviously much different than an on-the-spot agreement made by only those individuals who make a submission, for the specific submission being made. The exact delineation of distribution rights is likely to be institution specific and determined by a vigorous and contested discussion and negotiation beyond the scope of the IR staff. Many of the mandates that have been put into effect since early 2008 are based on the language first developed at Harvard for the Faculty of Arts and Sciences' mandate (see www.fas.harvard.edu/~secfas/February_2008_Agenda.pdf).

References and Suggested Readings

Albanese, Andrew. 2008. "Georgia State Sued Over E-reserves." *Library Journal* 133, no. 9: 16–17.

Cohen, Suzanne and Deborah Schmidle. 2007. "Creating a Multipurpose Digital Institutional Repository." *OCLC Systems & Services* 23, no. 3: 287–296.

Ferreira, Miguel, Eloy Rodrigues, Ana Alice Baptista, and Ricardo Saraiva. 2008. "Carrots and Sticks: Some Ideas on How to Create a Successful Institutional Repository." *D-Lib Magazine* 14, no. 1/2. Available: www.dlib.org/dlib/january08/ferreira/01ferreira.html (accessed January 17, 2009).

Fyffe, Richard and William C. Welburn. 2008. "ETDs, Scholarly Communication, and Campus Collaboration." *College & Research Libraries News* 69, no. 3: 152–155.

Hirtle, Peter B. 2006. "Author Addenda: An Examination of Five Alternatives." *D-Lib Magazine* 12, no. 11. Available: www.dlib.org/dlib/november06/hirtle/11hirtle.html (accessed January 27, 2009).

Jenkins, Barbara, Elizabeth Breakstone, and Carol Hixson. 2005. "Content In, Content Out: The Dual Roles of the Reference Librarian in Institutional Repositories." *Reference Services Review* 33, no. 3: 312–324.

Mercer, Holly, Brian Rosenblum, and Ada Emmett. 2007. "A Multifaceted Approach to Promote a University Repository: The University of Kansas' Experience." *OCLC Systems & Services* 23, no. 2: 190–203.

Palmer, Carole, Lauren C. Teffeau, and Mark P. Newton. 2008. *Identifying Factors of Success in CIC Institutional Repository Development: Final Report.* New York: The Andrew Mellon Foundation.

Reese, Terry. 2009. "Automated Metadata Harvesting: Low-Barrier MARC Record Generation from OAI-PMH Repository Stores Using MarcEdit." *Library Resources & Technical Services* 53, no. 2: 121–134.

Royster, Paul. 2007. "The Institutional Repository at the University of Nebraska–Lincoln: Its First Year of Operations." *OCLC Systems & Services* 23, no. 2: 183–189.

Increasing Use and Assessment

7

IN THIS CHAPTER:

- ✔ Metadata
- ✔ Register at All OAI Sites
- ✔ Increase Search Engine Rankings
- ✔ Increase Access Points
- ✔ Assessment
- ✔ Conclusion
- ✔ References

Regardless of the platform selected, an institutional repository (IR) is a significant financial investment. IR staff should be prepared to make the case for their project, in competition with many other worthy projects. As with any such project, assessment will be required to justify continued support by the institution. Fortunately, IRs by their very nature provide an effective and easy way to generate some quantitative assessment and demonstrate their impact: use statistics. Download numbers will help make the case for continued support by administration and for participation by the contributor pool, so taking steps to raise them is a fundamental part of repository management and development.

While increasing participation by contributors is likely to be the focus of efforts during the implementation stage, increasing use outside the institution will eventually need consideration. If the IR is to be successful in the typical goals of providing increased access and visibility and serving as a recruitment tool, IR managers need to take steps to maximize use of the content. While the simple act of posting the content will guarantee some use, it can be expanded by taking a few simple steps. By taking them, the institution's profile is enhanced, research's reach is extended, and the IR's goals are closer to fulfillment.

One way to maximize use is to ensure adequate indexing of the content, especially for nontextual material. Adequate indexing in turn means good metadata. A general principle for repository management is that the richer the metadata, the higher the use of repository content. Metadata can ensure higher use now and also enduring use because of its importance in preservation.

Another method to increase use is to ensure interoperability with traditional and developing systems and services that use specific standards to share content and information. For repositories, the most important standard is OAI-PMH. There are already a number of services that require compatibility with this standard (discussed later), so compliance should be a priority.

There are other ways to increase access points to repository content. Optimizing search engine indexing can be accomplished with a minimum of effort. The placement of links and search boxes on appropriate Web pages can help guide users to the IR. Catalog records for local and union catalogs may be warranted for some content and will provide another access point.

All of these techniques help increase the visibility and accessibility of a repository and thus its use. If they are implemented, when it comes time for assessment, numbers should be higher and the case for support more easily made. This is over and above the fact that scholarship and education are advanced as well.

Metadata

Metadata is often defined as data about data. It can help in the discoverability, or resource discovery, of the content in a repository. It also supports other aspects of repository management, such as administration and preservation. Metadata is commonly broken down into three types: descriptive, administrative, and structural. In addition, a combination of these types can be said to comprise preservation metadata. It is the first of these, descriptive, that plays the key role in aiding discoverability.

Descriptive Metadata and Resource Discovery

See the different standards used by Harvard University at **http://hul.harvard.edu/ois/digproj/metadata-standards.html#descriptive**.

For more information on Dublin Core, see **http://dublincore.org**.

Descriptive metadata contains basic information about a particular document or object such as the creator's name, the title, and the subject of the content. The way this information is entered and presented depends on the metadata standard being used. There are an overwhelming number of standards available, depending on the type of material being described, the community doing the description (e.g., library vs. information technology), and even geographic location. However, there is one essential standard that will satisfy basic needs and guarantee at least some discoverability: Dublin Core (Jones, 2007). Developed and maintained by the Dublin Core Metadata Initiative (DCMI), this standard is widely used. It comes, for example, preconfigured in the DSpace source code, and it is also used within Digital Commons. An essential aspect of Dublin Core is that it is compliant with OAI-PMH harvesting (discussed later).

Although full-text searching obviates some of the need for extensive descriptive metadata, there are reasons for adding descriptive metadata to content records. For one thing, internal search and sorting functions will require this information. For another, there may well be content types that are by definition not full-text searchable: audio files, photographs, paintings, etc. In addition, any text document that was not originally created electronically and has not been scanned so as to make the full text searchable will require descriptive metadata.

Metadata and Preservation

There is a role for metadata beyond the enhancement of content discoverability: content durability. Administrative and structural metadata are essential for this function. Administrative metadata determines such things as who can upload and remove a particular item, who can further edit its metadata, and who can have access to it. Structural metadata determines how items appear to a user. It is also used to keep separate elements of an item together. Some administrative and structural metadata are created as a part of the submission and posting process.

Elements of administrative and structural metadata combine to make up preservation metadata. The recognized standard for preservation metadata, including for IR content, is called *PREMIS*. It was developed by the PREMIS working group, which was sponsored by OCLC and the Research Libraries Group; it concluded its work in 2005. However, its main product, the PREMIS Data Dictionary for Preservation Metadata, has continued to be updated.

The PREMIS Data Dictionary for Preservation Metadata is available at **www.oclc.org/research/projects/pmwg**.

Preservation metadata can include information on the ownership or provenance of content, its authenticity, how it can be used (such as the programs necessary for viewing it), and any digital rights management issues (PREMIS Working Group, 2008). Preservation metadata is essential for a number of goals related to long-term access to repository content: protection from intentional or accidental damage, protection from loss or the loss of the relationships that bind together disparate elements of an item, tracking the technology required to view and use the content, maintaining proper access control over content with access restrictions, and maintaining the appearance and functionality of the original item. Institutional repositories promise perpetuity to contributors, and preservation metadata is a fundamental part of meeting that promise (Wheatley, 2004).

How Much Metadata?

Different people will have different answers to this question. Robert Tansley, creator of Eprints and developer at DSpace and now at Google, advises against spending much time on metadata for resource discovery, at least for full-text documents (Tansley, 2009). Although this might make librarians uncomfortable, his point that IR staff should be focusing their efforts on outreach instead is a valid one. Others will say that a rich set of metadata is essential not only for discovery but for preservation purposes as well (Wheatley, 2004) and that it is a fundamental responsibility of the repository to develop and maintain that metadata. These advocates have a valid point as well.

Practically, the level of metadata support will depend more on the staffing resources available to the institution than on any ideological position. In an ideal world, every repository would have the fullest set of metadata possible; in the real world, it will be necessary to settle for something less. If requirements are set too high, there is a risk that they will serve as an obstacle to content recruitment and processing, which serves no one well. There are already so many outside obstacles to IR success that building in an additional one in the form of overly demanding metadata requirements is a poor decision.

Nevertheless, as mentioned, a rich set of metadata has its place, especially for nontextual materials such as images, data files, and videos. This is another reason why it is important to have institutional support for the IR service and to have adequate resources dedicated to it. In particular, if the repository is to fulfill its purpose and promise as a reliable preservation service for valuable content, some administrative and structural metadata will be essential.

In summary, IR staff should push for as much metadata support as they can get from the institution but never use lack of that support as an excuse for not proceeding nor establish requirements that discourage participation. In the end, having content in the repository must take precedence over having "good" metadata.

Register at All OAI Sites

Google is not the only search engine. It is the most important one, of course, because this is what most people use to find what they are looking for. But Google suffers from some fundamental flaws, and a lot of people have put time and effort into developing other tools that overcome these flaws. The most exigent of these efforts for repository managers revolves around a metadata harvesting protocol called OAI-PMH.

The OAI in OAI-PMH

OAI is an acronym for Open Archives Initiative. OAI was begun in 2000, with the goal of using the Internet to link and unify the searching of repository content (Lagoze and Van de Sompel, 2001). In the words of its mission statement:

> The Open Archives Initiative develops and promotes interoperability standards that aim to facilitate the efficient dissemination of content. The Open Archives Initiative has its roots in an effort to enhance access to e-print archives as a means of increasing the availability of scholarly communication. (Open Archives Initiative Mission Statement at www.openarchives.org/OAI/OAI-organization.php)

OAI recognized the shortfalls of the existing methods of information dissemination: increased research and data creation; the slow pace of conventional publishing practices; and the economics behind the scholarly communication crisis whereby the price inflation of journal subscriptions outpaced the increase of library budgets, therefore requiring journal cancellations. It also recognized that some communities—particularly in physics, as represented by the disciplinary repository arXiv—had already begun to use the Internet to overcome some of these shortfalls. However, there was a clear need to ensure that these communities, and the new ones that were correctly expected to continue to develop at an increasing rate, could communicate with each other—in their parlance, be interoperable.

The PMH in OAI-PMH

In essence, OAI tasked itself with coming up with the structure necessary to provide that interoperability. The OAI originators wanted a solution that would be as easy to implement as possible, as cheaply as possible, so that as many information providers as possible could participate. What they came up with was the Protocol for Metadata Harvesting (PMH).

The protocol requires metadata to be made available in a common format, the Dublin Core Metadata Element Set. This metadata is encoded into XML, a prominent markup language. The metadata is then harvested, or gathered together, by various harvesters, or service providers. These harvesters contain only the metadata and provide a search tool for users to find the content in participating repositories. The metadata must therefore contain a link to the actual file in the repository.

Becoming OAI-PMH Compliant

Guidelines for making a repository compliant with OAI-PMH are available at www.openarchives.org/OAI/2.0/guidelines-repository.htm. Some technical skills are necessary, particularly a familiarity with XML. Once the necessary steps have been taken, the repository must go through conformance testing, which can be done at the OAI site. If the test is successful, the repository becomes registered. This is one area where commercial providers can provide an advantage, as they should be expected to make a repository compliant and see to it that it is registered.

Once a repository is registered, its contents become available for the service providers. The most well-known provider is OAIster (www.oaister.org), a service run by the University of Michigan Libraries, but there are many others. Repository staff can ensure their content is harvested by these providers by registering with them.

A list of service providers is available at **www.openarchives.org/service/listproviders.html**.

OAI-ORE

OAI's latest project has been to extend protocols to cover new types of content, defined as aggregations. Aggregations can include such things as bookmarks, online photo albums, documents that are packaged in different file formats, and other circumstantial, even ephemeral collections (Open Archives Initiative/Object Reuse and Exchange, 2008). ORE (Object Reuse and Exchange) seeks to gather together these various elements for machine readable use, essentially by creating a new resource and Universal Resource Indicator to keep the packages whole. ORE is still in its early stages, but, given the proliferation of these types of aggregations—every manifestation of Web 2.0 technology can be considered an aggregation—it promises to become an important part of the repository landscape.

There are diverse ways of keeping up to date with this development; several can be found at **www.openarchives.org/ore**.

Increase Search Engine Rankings

There is a great deal of speculation about how to rise in the rankings of major search engines (search engine optimization, or SEO) such as Google. Speculation is rampant because the actual search algorithms are proprietary and secret. Some say that it boils down to popularity and purchase, that is, rankings depend on how many other sites link to a given site

See Google's advice for improving ranking at **www.google.com/support/webmasters/bin/answer.py?answer=35769**.

and/or how much money has been paid to the search engine company. Certainly Google's PageRank™ does use linking as an essential element of its ranking. Search engines also depend on the ease of indexing any given site. The other important element of search engine ranking is content, which is analyzed and determined via numerous and complex variables.

One of the simplest things repository staff can do to improve the rankings of its content is to include a site map, or otherwise structure the site similar to a site map, for easy indexing. As search engine programs drill down through a site, this structure will help to ensure that all content is found. Also, sheer size helps. This is because as more links are built leading to content in the repository, the higher its standing, at least within Google's system. So another of the simplest and most effective ways to improve ranking is simply to continue to add content.

Increase Access Points

Having links to the repository does not just aid recruitment efforts, as discussed in Chapter 5, but it also helps build exposure to outside users. While opportunities may be few outside the institution, there are often multiple sites within the institution that make good entry points for the repository—institutional research pages, graduate school pages for those repositories that include theses and dissertations, and individual department and faculty pages are just a few examples. Failure to take advantage of these opportunities is more widespread than it ought to be (Jantz and Wilson, 2008) and is an easily remedied oversight. The proper sites for links will depend on the content in the repository, but every opportunity should be taken to identify them and have the link added.

Similarly, search boxes on various pages can lead users directly to content. Search boxes can be added on many of the pages within the library's site—such as pages for digital collections, online resources, library collections—to present the repository as a fundamental service and resource for the community.

Some content may warrant cataloging for inclusion in the library's catalog, state or regional union catalogs, and OCLC's WorldCat. For most, inclusion in one will mean easy inclusion in the others. Books and other monographs (Royster, 2007), technical reports, videos, and theses and dissertations all merit consideration for this treatment.

Assessment

Assessment is important for two reasons. First, it provides the basis for determining the success or failure of various repository management aspects; recruitment techniques, content priorities, and platform capabilities are the biggest of these. In this regard, assessment helps to redirect efforts for a more successful outcome. Second, because it is likely that a repository is competing for resources with other services or projects, assessment will be necessary to justify the required financial and personnel resources. Here, assessment aids in gaining continued support for the repository.

Assessment of the success of an IR can involve qualitative and quantitative measures. Quantitative measures could be of two basic types: uptake of the service by the contributor pool and use of the repository content by outsiders.

Quantitative Assessment

Uptake by the contributor pool can be calculated in a few ways, including by the percentage of individuals who have contributed at least one document, or by percentage of total research (or other material) per unit of time, probably a year, produced by the institution that is included in the repository (Xia and Sun, 2007). Early in the development of the repository, these measures are unlikely to be highly favorable. Alternatively, sheer numbers of documents included, or some measure of the uptake by organizational units (e.g., percentage of academic departments with some repository representation) can be used to better effect. One year should be the minimum amount of time before assessment is used to reflect true progress.

Use of the repository content can also document the value of the repository and justify its further support. This is why statistics are not just a value-added feature but are an essential component of any repository platform. The difficulty is that compiling download statistics can be problematic. For one thing, indexing by search engines artificially inflates the actual numbers, and currently only Digital Commons among all the platforms accounts for this in its statistics reporting. Furthermore, there is no established standard for an acceptable level of use of a repository. Comparisons can be made between repositories, but any internal benchmark will largely be arbitrary. Calculations can be made for downloads per item and cost per download, but these cannot be applied in the same way as similar information for journal use, for example, can be. This is because the use for repository content is for content created locally, so there are benefits to institutional authors and creators that are not taken into account in any mathematical calculation.

See **www.bepress.com/download_counts.html** for a fuller explanation of this problem.

Qualitative Assessment

Qualitative measures are more nebulous, but they are just as important. It is difficult to measure the value of such services as aiding a department's recruitment efforts, or generating goodwill from graduate students who are pleased to see download numbers, or easing a faculty member's life by providing a journal publishing platform and a peer-review tracking system. While quantifying satisfaction with such services is almost impossible, documenting it is not, and every opportunity to do so should be taken. In this regard, a survey of contributors can be conducted to track and demonstrate satisfaction.

Surveys can also provide feedback necessary to informed repositioning and repurposing of the repository. Flexibility in IR development has been stressed throughout this book, and feedback can help show in which directions IR staff should go to ensure maximum participation. In this regard, more informal methods of gathering comments, suggestions, and complaints should also be maintained. This may be done, for example, by gathering comments received via e-mail in the course of working with authors or via e-mail from a feedback link on the repository page. Such feedback then can be tracked via a wiki or other shared space. Repository staff tend to experience some turnover, and it is important to document institutional knowledge for the benefit of future managers and recruiters.

Other qualitative measures may focus not on user satisfaction but instead involve some measurement of the integration of the IR into the overall research and education program of the institution (Westell, 2006). Such integration may be assessed by the presence (or absence) of the repository in the governing and operating documents of the institution and its various divisions. These may include such documents as thesis and dissertation submission instructions and guidelines for compliance with grants.

One huge indicator of success would be the inclusion of repository participation as a requirement for the assessment of materials submitted for tenure and promotion decisions. This requirement is a clear indication that the institution has established the repository as a priority for all. Such an achievement marks an unparalleled success and should be the goal for all repositories.

Conclusion

As mentioned, there is no real conclusion to IR efforts. Increasing use and assessment will help define what directions staff should take to enhance the repository's visibility and effectiveness. The cycle then begins over again, marketing and expanding the reach of the IR, increasing use, and assessing progress. Each step is integral to any achievement of success, however it is defined.

A wide variety of IRs exists today. IRs continue to be established, and continuing pressure on library budgets, particularly in light of the economic crisis beginning in 2008, will only emphasize their usefulness and enhance their appeal. Getting started can be the most difficult step, and the decision to implement an IR does represent a significant, long-term commitment. Fortunately, there is a wide support group of practicing IR managers and staff and an increasing number of online and print resources to help guide newcomers. With the help of these resources, patience, and a lot of hard work, building an IR is possible.

References

Jantz, Ronald C. and Myoung C. Wilson. 2008. "Institutional Repositories: Faculty Deposits, Marketing, and the Reform of Scholarly Communication." *Journal of Academic Librarianship* 34, no. 3: 186–195.

Jones, Catherine. 2007. *Institutional Repositories: Content and Culture in an Open Access Environment.* Oxford: Chandos.

Lagoze, C. and H. Van de Sompel. 2001. "The Open Archives Initiative: Building a Low-Barrier Interoperability Framework." ACM/IEEE Joint Conference on Digital Libraries, pp. 54–62.

Open Archives Initiative Mission Statement. Available: www.openarchives.org/OAI/OAI-organization.php (accessed January 21, 2009).

Open Archives Initiative/Object Reuse and Exchange. 2008. "ORE User Guide—Primer." Available: www.openarchives.org/ore/1.0/primer (accessed January 17, 2009).

PREMIS Working Group. 2008. "Preservation Metadata for Digital Materials." Available: www.oclc.org/research/projects/pmwg/background.htm (accessed January 12, 2009).

Royster, Paul. 2007. "The Institutional Repository at the University of Nebraska–Lincoln: Its First Year of Operations." *OCLC Systems & Services* 23, no. 2: 183–189.

Tansley, Robert. 2009. "Presentation at Implementing an Institutional Repository: Benefits and Challenges." ALCTS workshop at ALA Midwinter, January 22.

Westell, Mary. 2006. "Institutional Repositories: Proposed Indicators of Success." *Library Hi Tech* 24, no. 2: 211–226.

Wheatley, Paul. 2004. "Institutional Repositories in the Context of Digital Preservation." *Microform & Imaging Review* 33, no. 3: 135–146.

Xia, Jingfeng and L. Sun. 2007. "Factors to Assess Self-Archiving in Institutional Repositories." *Serials Review* 33, no. 2: 73–80.

Seven Real-World Experiences in Establishing an Institutional Repository

II

DigitalCommons@ILR: Institutional Repository Marketing and Development at the Catherwood Library, ILR School, Cornell University

8

Mary J. Newhart, Suzanne A. Cohen, and James D. DelRosso

IN THIS CHAPTER:

Introduction

DigitalCommons@ILR is a multipurpose institutional repository (IR) for scholarship produced by the faculty in the Industrial and Labor Relations School (ILR) at Cornell University. Although it shares this purpose with many IRs, DigitalCommons@ILR sets itself apart in a number of ways. First, it was designed to function not only as a collection of faculty scholarly works but also as a subject-based IR for workplace-related information. Furthermore, unlike many IRs, it has been successfully integrated into the organization, receiving support from the school's administration and strong uptake from the faculty. Finally, it has routinely pushed the accepted boundaries for IRs by adopting a stance of flexibility: instead of creating a rigid and complicated set of policies, DigitalCommons@ILR adheres to easily adjustable guidelines so as to best meet the needs of its community. While a great deal of time and energy was initially spent choosing a technology platform, this case study focuses on the IR team's nontraditional approach to the IR's marketing and development.

For a discussion of the process we used in choosing a platform, see Cohen, S.A., and D.J. Schmidle. 2007. "Creating a Multipurpose Digital Institutional Repository." Available: **http://digitalcommons.ilr.cornell.edu/articles** (accessed December 22, 2008).

Background

The Catherwood Library, a unit within the Cornell University Library system, resides in and is funded by the ILR. In addition to its four-year undergraduate program and graduate programs focusing on workplace issues, ILR offers workshops and courses for professionals at extension sites throughout New York State. The ILR currently consists of 110 resident and extension faculty, and library staff work closely with these faculty through reference, instruction, and outreach services. The Catherwood Library collections, including the special collections housed in its Kheel Center for Labor–Management Documentation and Archives, serve as a comprehensive national resource for workplace-related information.

The committee that laid the groundwork for DigitalCommons@ILR was created out of a desire by the ILR to better promote the work of its faculty and researchers and the Catherwood Library's interest in obtaining and preserving scholarly information produced by ILR. Although this committee had the support of the ILR dean and representation from the library, faculty, and technical services, progress stalled until Catherwood hired a Web and Digital Projects Manager whose duties included the implementation of an IR. The Web and Digital Projects Manager formed a team from existing staff, drawing on expertise from Collection Development, Reference, Technical Services, and Information Technology.

The Need for Strategic Planning

From the beginning, the library team assigned to the IR project adopted the philosophy that, while the quality of the technology was important, the IR was only as good as its content. The team never believed the IR was a "build it and they will come" proposition. While faculty-created materials were the main concern, it quickly became evident that flexibility would be required to meet the immediate needs of Catherwood Library's entire community of patrons. As others have documented, when "transformational technologies are introduced in the conservative, controlled manner associated with stereotypical librarian culture its success can be hampered by organizational culture, often manifested by lengthy and complicated sets of policies" (Lindahl et al., 2008: 1). The IR team kept its focus on the best strategies for acquiring content rather than endless policy discussions.

The IR team decided that the vision and mission of the Catherwood Library would guide the building of the IR. As a tool that assists in furthering the goals of the library, the IR did not require its own mission or vision statement. Adopting this strategic approach removed the need to create separate policies and objectives for the IR and allowed for flexibility in meeting the needs of the school's faculty and staff. Additionally, it allowed the Catherwood librarians the opportunity to include subject-based collections that reflected the library's mission to provide "outstanding information and research services on all aspects of the world of work" (see www.ilr.cornell.edu/library/about/mission.html). The collections of workplace-related materials in the IR could strengthen the Catherwood Library's reputation as the most comprehensive resource of its type in North America.

The IR team also made the strategic decision to launch the IR before the marketing plan, policies, and procedures were in place. The IR team felt that the best way to approach the "transformational technology" was to experiment with and learn from it—to "jump in rather than wade in." Although this approach requires a culture that takes and accepts risks, it also creates opportunity for innovation and flexibility. Although some extra labor was involved when procedures/policies were changed midcourse to better meet the needs of users or to streamline staff workflow, there have been no regrets about choosing to build the internal infrastructure of the IR while simultaneously marketing and populating it with content.

Although a collection development policy was created and basic metadata was decided upon, the priority was given to the creation of a marketing plan for the IR. The decision to focus on internal marketing grew out of the strategic planning done by the IR project team. Based on experience gained from close working relationships with the faculty, the librarians recognized that many faculty members' lack of copyright knowledge, technological skill, and (most important) time would deter faculty from self-contribution of works to the IR. The marketing philosophy adopted by DigitalCommons@ILR reflected, and benefited from, this realization.

To view the DigitalCommons@ILR policy, see **http://digitalcommons.ilr.cornell.edu/dc_information/4**.

Adopting a Marketing Philosophy

The overall philosophy for the marketing plan was a simple one: focus on content. Knowing your audience is critical in the design of a marketing plan. In our case, we designed the plan for our internal audience, rather than external. Externally, the ILR and Catherwood Library were already well positioned as recognized experts in the field of workplace studies. Additionally, a powerful tool already existed that would find our content—Google. By creating recognition and support for DigitalCommons@ILR within the ILR, the team could grow the content of the IR, which would in turn build recognition and support both internally and externally.

In building the marketing plan to support this philosophy, the IR team identified the first step as winning support from the highest levels of the school's administration. The team sought and found a champion for the project within the school's leadership, solicited input from key faculty and staff, and sought feedback and advice from the broader Cornell University Library community. Catherwood Library's director then sought support for the project from the ILR dean, who, having already heard positive feedback, threw his full support behind it. The dean sent schoolwide e-mail communications encouraging participation and invited library staff to make a presentation at a full faculty meeting.

That meeting represented the second step in the marketing plan. To prepare, the IR team established a "representative sample" of documents to demonstrate the possibilities inherent in the IR by soliciting papers from the faculty and staff who had been previously contacted. Next, the IR team organized an educational session for the faculty administrative assistants, anticipating the need for their assistance in working with faculty. A DigitalCommons@ILR brochure was developed, and library staff liaisons were named to serve as a single point of contact for various ILR groups (e.g., resident faculty, extension faculty).

To access the DigitalCommons@ILR brocure, go to **http://digitalcommons.ilr.cornell.edu/dc_information/5**.

From contacts made during the first part of our marketing plan, we learned that the wider Cornell University Library had adopted the goal of improving scholarly communications by educating faculty on copyright retention and open access initiatives. We adopted this goal for Digital Commons@ILR, and our presentation to the faculty reflected this purpose in its focus on the issues surrounding copyright in scholarly communication. The faculty meeting, one year after the launch of the IR, was a turning point in terms of participation: afterward, many faculty expressed interest in getting their works into DigitalCommons@ILR.

The third step of the marketing plan was to reach out and respond to those faculty members who expressed an interest in participating. Early on, the IR team had determined that it would be necessary for the library to commit to doing much of the work involved in getting a document into the IR. While this case study does not focus on staffing issues, the importance of adequate staffing to meet this commitment should not be underestimated (see Cohen and Schmidle, 2007). The marketing message was effective because the IR team stressed the efficiency and ease of using the IR: the only thing that faculty needed to remember is that DigitalCommons@ILR existed and they needed only to contact the library to have their content included. Repetition of this simple message in a variety of formats turned out to be a very powerful tool.

Finding a Champion and Building Support

Early in the planning process, the IR team solicited advice and participation from ILR staff and faculty who could benefit from DigitalCommons @ILR. The team also searched for and found a champion for the project in an associate dean, who saw the IR as a potential marketing and outreach tool for the school. By reaching out to other departments, we learned that the IR might also prove useful in meeting several ongoing needs outside of the library.

For example, the ILR's Web development group needed to manage the growing use of the school's Web site as a place to post copies of faculty articles and papers. The IR offered a "managed system" to not only post papers but also provide proper copyright management. By soliciting the input of this group early on, a procedure was created that required any faculty or staff member wishing to upload an article or paper to contact the library IR team.

Similarly, the *Industrial and Labor Relations Review*, a leading interdisciplinary journal published by ILR, had been looking to establish an online presence. When it was determined that DigitalCommons@ILR had the required functionality, the Catherwood Library was able to provide the journal an online home at no additional cost to the ILR *Review*. In exchange, Catherwood received blanket permission to post articles written by participating faculty members that were published in the ILR *Review*.

A third example of building support involves the Employment and Disability Institute (EDI), which provides continuing education and technical assistance on many aspects of disability in the workplace. The EDI wished to make available online and index its many publications, including material produced from grants where the granting agencies required open access. DigitalCommons@ILR met many of the Institute's requirements, but EDI also desired a more seamless retrieval of documents stored in DigitalCommons@ILR from links on their own Web site. This led to the creation of a taxonomy that is used during the intake process to index all of their content in DigitalCommons@ILR, allowing for both keyword and subject browsing from the EDI's Web site of DigitalCommons@ILR collections (see www.ilr.cornell.edu/edi).

Measuring Success

When claiming success in a venture, it is vital to be clear in your criteria. While we did not set any particular participation goal at the start of the IR implementation, we are very pleased with the fact that scholarship from 68 percent of the ILR's faculty is represented in DigitalCommons @ILR. The strategic decision making and marketing plan described earlier seems to have successfully addressed many of the reasons that faculty cite for nonparticipation in IRs, including the learning curve, confusion with copyright, and concerns about whether posting a manuscript constitutes "publishing" (Davis and Connolly, 2007). The IR team's willingness to act as consultants when faculty have questions about copyright and publisher contracts has increased participation and helped educate the faculty about broader scholarly communication issues. The better that faculty understand issues of copyright, the easier it will be to lawfully deposit their materials in the IR in the future. Of course, being encouraged by the school's deans to participate is a powerful incentive for the faculty and has greatly contributed to our success. Anecdotally, faculty currently participating are pleased with the extra exposure their work is receiving (they tell us that they are being contacted more often by journalists and others outside of the school), and they enjoy receiving the regular usage statistics that the Digital Commons platform provides to authors. As such, "word of mouth" by participating faculty is helping to spread interest among nonparticipants.

But we also measure our success in the ways that DigitalCommons@ILR benefits the Catherwood Library and the ILR beyond the traditional IR mission of housing faculty scholarly works. The expanded scope of our collection has allowed the library to assume an integrated marketing role both internally and externally: we provide an outlet for not only faculty but also institutions and groups within the school who wish to disseminate their work, and we also promote the library itself as a premier source of workplace-related information online.

DigitalCommons@ILR provides support for a number of departments within the school and the library. As noted, the IR team now assesses the state of copyright permissions for all documents posted to the ILR Web site, which both assists the school's Web team and demonstrates the value that libraries can supply to organizations involved in online document dissemination. The IR team plays an important role in collection development, providing a place to store and deliver born-digital documents that would have traditionally been added to our print collection if available in that format.

Furthermore, we are always looking for new ways to assess the impact DigitalCommons@ILR is having on the library and the school. We track both hits and full-text downloads, for the entire IR and for specific series, and invite feedback from participating faculty and institutions (at the time of writing, the IR has had over 1.3 million full-text downloads). We're also exploring ways to interact more with the end users of the document and get them more invested in the IR. These efforts parallel our drive to keep the IR current in terms of technology, and both are described next.

The Future

DigitalCommons@ILR is an established and successful IR implementation for Catherwood Library and the ILR. As such, it has moved from being a transformative technology to an established technology. The library, with support of the ILR's administration, has made a commitment to maintain the IR, to grow the IR, and to provide a high level of personalized service to faculty and staff. In order to continue its development, staffing levels will need to be maintained and possibly expanded, time must be allotted for further experimentation and innovation, and plans for longer term preservation need to be developed.

We also realize that becoming an established technology leaves Digital Commons@ILR vulnerable to obsolescence. As such, an IR team priority is to keep abreast of new developments and trends in the field of digital assets management. Exploring new possibilities—such as user profiles and folksonomies—will allow us to keep DigitalCommons@ILR current and facilitate the continued development of an involved and vibrant online community of patrons. Building on our earlier successes, the IR team is ready to start another round of strategic planning and marketing to meet these new challenges, using a philosophy that embraces risk and flexibility.

References

Cohen, S.A. and D.J. Schmidle. 2007. "Creating a Multipurpose Digital Institutional Repository." Available: http://digitalcommons.ilr.cornell.edu/articles (accessed December 22, 2008).

Davis, P.M., and M.J.L. Connolly. 2007. "Institutional Repositories: Evaluating the Reasons for Non-use of Cornell University's Installation of DSpace." *D-Lib Magazine* 13, no. 3/4. Available: www.dlib.org/dlib/march07/davis/03davis.html (accessed January 13, 2009).

Lindahl, David, Suzanne Bell, Susan Gibbons, and Nancy Fried Foster. 2008. "Institutional Repositories, Policies, and Disruption." Available: http://hdl.handle.net/1802/3865 (accessed December 22, 2008).

Implementing an Institutional Repository Using DigiTool: The Colorado State University Experience

9

Dawn Bastian Paschal

IN THIS CHAPTER:

Introduction

The Colorado State University Libraries (CSUL) has managed a repository of digital institutional assets since 2000–2001, when it sought to enhance access to images from its renowned International Poster Collection and popular Garst Wildlife Photographic Collection. Since that time, the repository has grown to include an additional six collections spanning historical documents and maps; agricultural industries and organizations; reports on water resources development and water supply; oral histories; award-winning student research projects; and historical collections focusing on individuals. As this resource expanded, so did staff knowledge, understanding, and recognition of the technical, organizational, and cultural challenges of developing an institutional repository (IR). When Colorado State University (CSU) included deployment of an IR in its strategic plan for research and discovery, CSUL was an experienced and enthusiastic leader and partner in the effort to ensure digital products of campus research and teaching are accessible far into the future.

Setting

CSU is a public, land-grant institution founded as the Colorado Agricultural College in 1870, six years before the Colorado Territory gained statehood. Located in Fort Collins, about 60 miles north of Denver, CSU's enrollment is currently about 26,000, and extramural funding exceeds $300 million annually. As a university with a Carnegie designation of Research University/VH (very high research activity), CSU is a leader in science and technology research, particularly in infectious diseases, environmental science, clean energy technologies, and atmospheric science. CSU's exceptional professional programs include veterinary medicine (ranked second in the nation by *U.S. News and World Report*), construction management, journalism and technical communication, occupational therapy, and agriculture. The CSU system also includes CSU–Pueblo, a satellite campus of more than 4,000 students situated in the Pikes Peak region of southern Colorado, and the online CSU–Global Campus. The latter premiered in September 2008 and has a total enrollment of 1,050.

CSUL includes Morgan Library and two branch libraries that support the Atmospheric Science Department and the College of Veterinary Medicine and Biomedical Sciences. Print holdings total more than 2 million books, bound journals, and government documents. More than 30,000 electronic resources are accessible from CSUL's Web site, which has grown rapidly in size and complexity since the late 1990s. This includes books, journals, and locally digitized reports, posters, slides, photographs, oral histories, and other primary resource materials.

IR Pilot Project

The author of this chapter, who was the Coordinator for Bibliographic Control and Electronic Resource Services, became the Coordinator for Metadata and Digital Services and is now the Coordinator for Digital Repositories Services.

In 2004, the Dean of Libraries charged the Coordinator for Bibliographic Control and Electronic Resource Services and the Physical Sciences Librarian with developing a pilot IR project using the CSUL's existing digital repository and award-winning undergraduate research from CSU's annual Celebrate Undergraduate Research and Creativity Showcase event. They met with the competition's coordinator, a professor from the Chemistry Department, to garner support and gather information. She proved to be very enthusiastic about the project and gave excellent feedback on how to encourage voluntary repository submissions from the approximately 20–30 entries honored as prize winners. A permissions form was developed for both students and their faculty mentors to use when depositing the projects, all of which are poster sessions.

The success of the pilot was mixed. Deposits in 2004 numbered 12; there were 13 in 2005 and 7 in 2006. The librarians working on the pilot agreed there were two possible reasons for the low numbers. First, the competition is held in April, not long before finals begin in May, and students and faculty are busy preparing for the end of the semester. Second, there was no tool available for direct online submission of projects when entering the competition. However, students who did deposit were enthusiastic about making their research openly available on the Internet and understood the value of doing so. The CSUL promoted the idea of sharing CSU research and scholarship online and demonstrated it could manage an IR project on a small scale. In addition, staff gained knowledge about intellectual property issues, marketing and promotion of an open access repository, and recognition of the effort that would be required to build a new culture of scholarly communication on campus.

Strategic Planning and the IR

In 2005, the CSU assigned responsibility for creating "a digital archive to preserve and make accessible institutional assets" to the Senior Vice

President/Provost, the Dean of Libraries, the Dean of the Graduate School, and the Council of Research Deans in its 2006–2015 strategic plan. The proposed timeline included a three-year phased implementation beginning in FY2006. CSU was particularly eager to use an IR to launch an electronic thesis and dissertation (ETD) submission program, but there was also great interest in archiving and sharing faculty preprints and postprints, research data, portfolios, conference papers, gray literature, public policy documents, and other materials.

To view this plan, go to **www.president.colostate.edu/strategicplanning/pages/pdf/march06_fullplan.pdf**.

As CSUL was the designated leader of this project, development of the repository was included as an objective in its own strategic plan. A team composed of representatives from various CSUL departments (Reference and Instruction, Metadata and Digital Services, University Archives and Special Collections, and Library Technology Services) was charged with developing a formal project description planning document.

Preliminary Decision Making

The decision to create an IR at CSU happened concurrently with a librarywide reorganization. A separate Digital Repositories Services Department was created with the reallocation of two faculty librarian positions from the Metadata and Digital Services Department. The CSUL decided it needed to hire one additional staff member for the new department, so recruitment began in early 2007 for a Digital Repositories Librarian; existing vacancies were combined to fund this position. The CSUL acknowledged that additional staff would probably be needed in the future following growth of the repository.

CSUL was already using the CONTENTdm® digital collection management software to successfully manage its own repository of locally digitized collections and was pleased with both the product and company support. However, it decided to formally investigate the possibility of using other software, as CONTENTdm® was initially developed to handle images primarily, and it lacked some of the functionality of true IR software. For the campus repository, CSUL felt it would need something more powerful and with additional features.

CSUL naturally decided to offer CSU–Pueblo an invitation to showcase its research, scholarship, and primary resource materials in its own collection within the IR. This proposal was eagerly accepted. As the library at CSU–Pueblo is small, greatly lacking in resources, and did not yet have any digital repository of its own, library staff there knew that a collaborative effort was key to its ability to preserve and provide access to its intellectual assets.

Development of the IR

Software Evaluation and Selection

In late 2006, the Coordinator for Digital Repositories Services and the Coordinator for Library Technology Services were charged with a broad review of current digital repository packages available. Prior to starting, they compiled the following checklist of locally required system features:

- Standards based
- Interoperable with other systems and services
- Ability to reuse and re-purpose content
- Ability to store, access, display, and manage multiple formats (text, video, audio, images, learning objects, etc.)
- Ability to define item types in addition to those that come with the system
- Ability to post an item, URL, or agent (executable file)
- Ability for items of multiple types to be linked together and accessible as one item (e.g., faculty research notes, a draft, preprint, and final article)
- Ingest single or multiple objects with ease
- Easily customized, simple to use interface (for both staff and users)
- Flexible support of metadata schemes
- Easily customized metadata templates for document description, with automatic extraction of metadata from files whenever possible
- Generate statistical reports
- Audit trail for all objects (date of posting, number of accesses, modifications, etc., and by whom)
- High level of granularity for permissions
- Ability to limit access at object and collection levels
- Ability to perform simple and advanced searches, place limits on searches
- Ability to search across all collections in repository
- Ability to publish journals

The following system features were identified as desirable:

- Platform independence (can run on a variety of operating systems)
- SQL-compatible database
- Ability to retain customized screens following release and installation of new versions
- Display of brief or full record view
- Unicode built in to handle vernacular scripts

After considering several open source and vendor packages, an in-depth evaluation of two was conducted: DSpace and DigiTool. A sales representative from the Ex Libris Group traveled to CSUL to present the DigiTool product, and the two coordinators attended conferences and consulted journal articles to learn more about both DSpace and DigiTool. Phone interviews were conducted with institutions that had implemented these platforms, using a standard set of questions appropriate to each product. Because most published comparisons of IR software at the time focused almost exclusively on features and cost, and very little was documented about supportability and usability, our user questions focused on these two areas.

Following review, the coordinators concluded that both DigiTool and DSpace were viable solutions for CSU. A vanilla, out-of-the box implementation could be accomplished with both products using existing staff resources. However, in utilizing DigiTool, CSUL could implement for users a more powerful, more sophisticated product with greater functionality and a lesser commitment of staff time. To achieve the level of functionality that DigiTool had, the coordinators estimated it would take at least one programmer one year of effort—possibly two—to customize DSpace. In addition, DigiTool could integrate easily with two Ex Libris products CSUL was already running: its link resolver, SFX®, and its federated search/metasearch application, known as MetaLib®. For these reasons, DigiTool was recommended over DSpace, and the Dean of Libraries approved its purchase in early 2007.

Development of Policies and Guidelines

Following selection of DigiTool as an IR platform for CSU, CSUL formed a Repositories Matrix Team responsible for general managerial oversight of both the DigiTool and CONTENTdm® repositories. Chaired by the Coordinator for Digital Repositories Services, members included the coordinators of University Archives and Special Collections, College Liaisons, Metadata and Preservation Services, Research and Development, and Library Technology Services. The team was sponsored by the Assistant Dean for Digital Services, reported to her and the other members of the CSUL administrative group, and provided regular updates to CSUL's Planning Group, which consisted of all coordinators and the CSUL administration. Its general charge included the following:

- Develop guidelines for establishing digital repositories.
- Guide the development of definitions of service models for repositories.
- Provide input to plans for repositories.
- Develop collection and metadata policies for repositories.
- Create specifications for user (public and staff) interfaces.
- Participate in the development of tools and their testing for repositories.
- Offer training to CSUL staff.
- Develop sessions to train the trainers for users of repositories.
- Provide advice on marketing strategies for repositories.
- Devise evaluations for repositories and participate in their conduct and review.

- Provide advice on collaborations for repositories that involve external organizations.
- Communicate team progress to and invite comment from CSUL staff members.

The members of the Repositories Matrix Team began investigating, defining, developing, and recommending policies and guidelines for the repository. Existing policies created by other institutions were used for guidance, and input and review were sought from appropriate staff within CSUL. CSUL's Planning Group gave final approval to all policies and guidelines before they were posted on the IR's Web site.

The team first drafted a document outlining general policies and guidelines, which includes sections on content scope; authorship/creation; author, creator, and university rights; nature of works; file formats accepted for deposit; access; and withdrawal of items; plus other information. Metadata would remain visible for withdrawn items to those who already have the persistent URL, but neither the work nor its metadata would be available for searching or harvesting by Internet search engines.

The team was careful to state that material included in the IR should be products of research and scholarship or that which document the history and intellectual life of the institution. All theses and dissertations would be accepted, as CSUL is the official archive of these items, but other student works must be recognized as award winners or deemed suitable for long-term preservation and access by a faculty member.

The preservation and format support policy documents the CSUL's commitment to and provision of preservation support for specific file formats at the outset of the IR. While CSUL pledged to monitor format changes and migrate items from one file format to a succeeding format when necessary and possible, it wished to be cautious and not promise more than it may someday be able to deliver. Based heavily on the University of Michigan's policy for its Deep Blue repository, CSUL's delineates three levels of support: greatest, limited, and minimal. As the level of preservation support provided for a repository contribution is determined by the file format in which it is submitted, users are advised to consult the *Registered Formats and Support Levels* table that is included when deciding which format to use. As new formats and standards emerge, and its experience with digital preservation grows, the CSUL will review and update this table and the entire policy.

The *Registered Formats and Support Levels* table is available at **http://lib.colostate.edu/repository/preservation.html**.

The Repositories Matrix Team also shared in the development of an informative Web site for the IR. In addition to the policies mentioned earlier, team members drafted a FAQ sheet and information on copyright and services for authors/creators. The Associate Dean for Digital Services worked closely with university legal counsel to develop a deposit agreement.

See **http://lib.colostate.edu/repository** for information about the repository; for the interface for the repository itself, see **http://digitool.library.colostate.edu**.

Implementation and Project Management

The three members of Digital Repositories Services and the three members of Research and Development collaborated directly for about five months in 2007 to implement the DigiTool software, following training provided by Ex Libris. One staff member from Library Technology Services attended the training also, as did three from CSU–Pueblo. Initially meetings were held twice a week, then daily before being gradually phased out.

Progress was carefully tracked using the CSUL's internal wiki, visible only to staff, and an online tool called *Flyspray*. Generally, project plan details, meeting minutes, decisions, and action items were recorded in the wiki. All tasks, plus priorities, issues, problems, and concerns associated with them were thoroughly documented in Flyspray. These tools were invaluable to tracking and managing the implementation process.

The team was also responsible for customizing the user interface. This was successfully accomplished without conflicts from DigiTool service packs, and it was made reasonably compliant with existing library and university requirements and standards (header, footer, page layout, logos, color scheme, fonts, styles, and Google Analytics tracking codes). Initially, customizations were applied to the interfaces to all other modules (Management, Approver, Collection Management, Deposit, Web Ingest), but Research and Development found that changes needed to be made to a directory and/or template file to prevent overwrites. DigiTool later added links to more easily navigate among staff modules, which removed some of the need to customize them. Eventually the team decided that customizing the staff modules was not worth the extra effort, although the Deposit module may be customized should our clientele wish to start using it.

Metadata

The CSUL has a tradition of building rich, full metadata for discovery and management of both its print and digital collections. The implementation of the IR underscored the need for an updated and expanded metadata policy. For example, should there be a MARC record in the catalog for anything that lives in the repository? When should a MARC record in the catalog be repurposed for a repository item, and when should another metadata schema be used? Should Library of Congress Subject Headings terms and/or keywords be assigned to materials in the IR, or is full-text searching adequate for object discovery and retrieval?

The Coordinator for Digital Repositories Services decided that existing MARC records from the catalog should be repurposed for the IR whenever possible, for reasons of efficiency. One exception is the ETDs. The ETD-MS schema, based on Dublin Core (DC), is richer and fuller than DC and allows the inclusion of important metadata elements that DC and MARC do not. These include information about degrees and thesis and dissertation committee members, both important to generating reports that would be of interest to faculty and campus administrators.

The majority of works deposited in the CSU IR do not have MARC records in the catalog, so metadata is built for them using DC. As the CSUL found when building its CONTENTdm® repository, this schema is simple and concise, yet easily refined with qualifiers for application to more complex materials. The Metadata Encoding and Transmission Standard (METS) is used for compound digital objects. Because DigiTool supports multiple metadata schemas, and interest has been expressed in putting some materials from the Art Department in the repository, it is likely that additional schema will be used in the future.

Marketing and Promotion

The members of Digital Repositories Services worked closely with the Assistant to the Dean for Grant Writing and Marketing in developing and executing a plan for initial marketing and promotion of the IR. The Digital Repositories Librarian collaborated with her to produce a brochure that could be distributed at presentations and by the College Liaisons at meetings with their colleges and departments. An entire issue of the *Library Connection* newsletter was devoted to IRs. The Coordinator of Digital Repositories Services gave a presentation about the IR initiative to the college deans and the Faculty Council Committee on Libraries. She also attended department meetings with the liaison for the College of Applied Human Sciences, where she spoke about the repository.

Marketing and promotion efforts were carried out from mid-2007 throughout 2008. In mid-2008, the Assistant to the Dean for Grant Writing and Marketing left her position, which has since been filled. The Coordinator for Digital Repositories will be working with her replacement on an updated marketing and promotion plan.

Populating the CSU IR

The Coordinator for Digital Repositories Services developed a preliminary plan for populating the IR in consultation with the other members of the Repositories Matrix Team, the College Liaisons, and the Libraries Planning Group. Obviously, the first step would be to target the "low-hanging fruit" that could be deposited quickly and with ease: materials that were born digital or were already in digital form and were in the public domain or otherwise free of copyright restrictions. The first items that came to mind were CSU publications and the Celebrate Undergraduate Research and Creativity student research projects already stored in the CSUL's CONTENTdm® repository. The university owned the copyright to the former, and the CSUL already had permission to distribute the student projects on the Internet. As the CSUL was also developing plans for a pilot ETD submission project, permission to distribute those documents would be secured as well. Other material would be gathered from "early adopters" identified during the normal course of work or through marketing efforts.

A small number of items were first deposited in mid-2007, primarily for testing purposes. During the same timeframe, the Atmospheric Science Department signaled an interest in preserving and making digital copies of its Atmospheric Science papers series available in the repository. Known as "Bluebooks," these are frequently requested by researchers, and the department was working on a project to retrospectively digitize as many titles as possible. The CSUL was given approximately 250 titles to deposit. In addition, some students voluntarily deposited their ETDs, and one of the College Liaisons worked with a graduate student to secure presentations from the Forest Biomass Conference that was held on campus. CSUL downloaded publications from the Colorado Water Resources Research Institute's Web site into the IR and deposited some papers and reports from Civil Engineering.

Campus interest in the IR continued to grow. For example, a professor of Animal Science and renowned designer of livestock handling facilities asked that materials posted on her Web site be archived in the IR. Both the Shortgrass Steppe (SGS) Long Term Ecological Research Project (LTER) and the College of Engineering indicated they have databases they would like to link to items in the repository. In addition, Research Services signaled an interest in conducting a pilot project using legacy data sets from Atmospheric Science. However, it is clear that the current scholarly communications culture will need to change to dramatically increase the number of deposits by other campus units. Librarians are finding that, while other faculty would like to self-archive past publications in the repository, they are often unable to do so in a manner consistent with copyright, as they have not saved their preprints or postprints.

The CSU IR Two Years Later

As of January 2009, CSU's IR contains 3,444 items organized into eight of nine top-level collections and 38 subcollections. These are further divided by category (faculty publications, technical bulletins, seminar papers, etc.) or date. Items deposited include published articles, presentations, journals, images, audio and video files, and other materials. The CSUL also deposits the primary resource materials it digitizes to support teaching and research, and those collections that reside in its CONTENTdm® repository will eventually be migrated to DigiTool.

An analysis of downloads reveals that two of the most popular items in the repository are undergraduate student research projects from the CURC Showcase. The two journals deposited, *Journal of Student Affairs*, published by the Student Affairs in Higher Education graduate program, and *Furthering Perspectives*, issued by the Anthropology Graduate Student Society, are also widely popular. Two other items with the highest number of downloads are a memoir of a local water engineer and a master's thesis from the History Department about the Fort Collins Mormon community.

Conclusion

CSUL was well-positioned to partner with other campus units to create an IR. During the past two years, it has utilized its knowledge and experience to successfully implement, develop, and promote this important new resource. Now that it contains a solid base of materials on which to build, and is drawing more and more attention, the time is right to focus on aggressively marketing the repository, securing more content, and working to address issues with the culture of scholarly communication at the university.

Implementing an Institutional Repository:

The Process in the Small College Environment at Macalester College

Janet C. Sietmann and Teresa A. Fishel

10

Introduction

Macalester College, in St. Paul, Minnesota, successfully established an institutional repository (IR) in 2005. We were able to implement and populate our repository in a very short period of time. We faced many challenges during the process, and we hope by sharing our experiences that other institutions find a potential road map for their own efforts. We highlight how we went about planning, populating, developing policies, promoting, and maintaining our IR. Before we explain our process, we think it's important to discuss what an IR means in a small college environment and, more important, why we believe libraries should be a major player in campus publishing. The IR is not the only digital scholarship initiative that Macalester is currently managing. Macalester is involved in several consortium projects, including REALIA (www.realiaproject.org) and a CLIC consortium project using CONTENTdm® to manage images. This chapter focuses only on the text-based IR at Macalester College.

IN THIS CHAPTER:

CLIC (Cooperating Libraries in Consortium) is our collaborative group for managing our integrated library system; see **www.clic.edu**.

Who We Are

Macalester College is a four-year, undergraduate liberal arts college in St. Paul, Minnesota. The current student population is approximately 1,900, with 32 percent from the Midwest, 57 percent from other states, and 11 percent international from 68 countries. Currently 48 out of the 50 United States are represented in the student body. There are 164 full-time faculty. Library staff number 19, not including Web services and media services personnel who are members of the planning group.

Our faculty are prolific authors and publish in all disciplines. Our students work closely with our faculty, and many are coauthors on published articles. This environment provides us with a wealth of opportunities to populate our IR. We decided early in the process that we wanted to focus on preservation and promotion of faculty publications

Faculty research pages with a list of their publications are located under Selected Works at **http://digital commons.macalester.edu/sw_ gallery.html**.

in a digital environment. However, our initial efforts to develop an IR began as a result of a challenge we had in providing access to our senior honors projects (which we will discuss later). We saw an IR as an opportunity to address the specific challenge of providing wider and more open access to our honors projects while at the same time showcasing and preserving both our student and faculty research and publications. Rapid changes in the electronic environment contributed to considering a new service to address both research and publishing needs.

Change in Scholarly Work and the Transition to Library as Publisher

In 2005, the library established the strategic goal of becoming the gateway and comprehensive information center in support of research and instruction at Macalester College. As we focused on transitioning our collections from print to digital, we took a leading role in developing the IR for campus publications. This focus came at a time when developments in open access were providing new opportunities for publishing activities. The library was seeking opportunities to both preserve and promote unique publications by the Macalester community. Opportune timing and suitable systems provided the foundations we needed to establish ourselves as publishers as well as preservationists.

Planning

For many years the development and use of images for classroom teaching and research projects was done independently by individual faculty and staff. It was clear, however, that a campuswide solution was needed for storing, cataloging, and managing digital images. Especially faculty who had been part of early grant-funded technology initiatives, such as REALIA, became involved. In 2004, we formed the Digital Assets Management (DAM) group, consisting of staff from the library, media services, Web services, and Information Technology Services (ITS).

DAM held a brainstorming meeting and clustered resulting ideas into five categories: planning; outreach and education; partnerships and grants; work processes; and content. Planning was done with the entire group. We determined the best software to manage and provide access to digital images. We considered platforms, outsourcing, stakeholders, access, copyright, scanning, and maintenance. Committee members attended many conferences and workshops to gather information on institutional repositories. We researched standards and metadata schemes to ensure our projects would be high quality and long lasting.

The marketing subgroup performed outreach and education. It was charged with spreading the word about repositories and their usefulness. Marketing was also responsible for recruiting faculty (early adopters and those willing to be part of pilot projects) and for surveying the campus on perceived repository needs.

In the area of partnerships and grants, we explored partnering with others such as CLIC and the Minnesota Oberlin Group. The library director worked with the Development Office to research grant opportunities, although none were available to meet our needs at that time.

When we looked at work processes, we knew the ideal staffing solution would be to hire someone whose primary responsibility would be the IR. However, this was not possible given budget constraints. Therefore, the current Reserves supervisor was asked to function as the repository coordinator. This seemed a good match, because the tasks involved in adding and managing content for both systems were somewhat similar. The library director believed the IR initiative was vital to the library's role on campus and that resources should be devoted to that project. To accommodate the added work of the IR, a library student manager was trained to handle many of the Reserves processing duties.

Content was, of course, the heart and soul of the IR initiative. DAM brainstormed a list of about 50 projects that we thought would be likely candidates for a repository and would provide solutions or content management for various campus constituencies. These prospective projects included college publications, faculty meeting minutes, student papers, and archives of photographs and music. Student honors projects were chosen as our first project. They are of high quality and are cataloged in OCLC and in our consortium catalog, CLICnet. They are in demand both on campus and through interlibrary loan. We needed to make the projects available for research purposes, but they were shelved in the archives, which has limited access.

We developed a master plan to guide the processes of creating, collecting, and managing content produced by the Macalester College community. The latest version of "Digital Collections Master Plan: Content, Systems, Access and Comprehensive Framework" can be found at http://digitalcommons.macalester.edu/annrep/4.

The Minnesota Oberlin Group consists of the libraries of Carleton College, Gustavus Adolphus College, College of St. Benedict/St. John's University, St. Olaf College, and Macalester College; the group collaborates on solutions to common issues, best practices, and resource and information sharing. Information is available at **www.macalester.edu/mnobe/**.

Platform

We developed a list of criteria for our platform choice, evaluated several platforms, and selected one in May 2005. Among our criteria was a platform to provide for a quick start in managing text content and for outsourcing the technical side. Outsourcing was necessary because, even though we were partnering with ITS, ITS couldn't provide technical support as they were managing the installation of our new campus administrative system at the time. The college was willing to pay for outsourcing the IR in lieu of hiring new staff.

Other important criteria for us were a self-deposit feature and a journal component. Self-deposit allows honors students and other authors to upload their own scholarship in just a few minutes. The repository coordinator does not need to scan documents. With a journal component we can produce an online journal with all the publishing features, including submitting, reviewing, editing, and managing submissions electronically.

We chose bepress' Digital Commons platform. Our vendor license includes setup, training, support, documentation, upgrades, and hosting, all for a reasonable cost. Pricing is confidential. Bepress has been very accommodating to our requests for customization and has been impressively responsive to all our needs.

Promoting

How do we get the word out? We build relationships, we solicit deposits, and we have conversations. One-on-one contact with faculty and students has been our most effective promotion, and we are planning further promotional activities. The following are some examples of the ways in which we have promoted and encouraged the use of our IR.

Honors students are asked to submit their projects to Digital Commons, but they require constant reminders and help. Even after graduation, we continue to seek their submissions if they have given permission for their projects to be included but have not submitted them. For those needing help with the self-submit process, we upload projects for them. Recently, a publisher contacted us to obtain permission to reproduce part of one graduate's honors project in a forthcoming book. We were able to use the SPARC author's addendum so that the graduate would retain her rights and we could keep the honors project in the IR.

We collaborate with the Academic Programs office, which oversees the entire honors projects program: setting the timeline, making sure deadlines are met, and conferring final approval. Academic Programs provides us with spreadsheets that contain student author names, departments, project titles, and faculty advisors. They also produce a book of abstracts that our catalogers use to aid in creation of MARC records to be displayed in our local catalog and in OCLC.

The reference librarians have a formal program in place during the Fall and the Spring terms to inform honors students of the specialized services and resources available to them as honors students. At these sessions, the repository coordinator talks to students about copyright, about seeking permission when necessary, and about the benefits of OA.

In addition to the honors projects, we add the papers of students who have received awards at conferences. Notices of these are published in the *Bulletin*, our biweekly official campus newsletter. Students and their faculty advisors are then contacted to obtain permission to deposit their papers in the IR.

Faculty support is critical in promoting the IR. We worked with early adopters on projects and introduced the IR in our semiannual library representatives meeting (one representative from each academic department). Most faculty are enthusiastic about showcasing the work of their students. For example, Professor Bill Moseley in the Geography Department tells his students: "This is an important way of sharing your insights with the broader scholarly community (and it is another way of giving back—and moving away from a model of extractive research). I really hope you will share your honors theses in this format—in addition to the traditional paper copy." We have put Professor Moseley's quote on our main IR page, and we believe it has influenced students to contribute their projects. Through promoting, we increased our participation from eight selected honors projects in 2005 to 75 percent of all honors projects produced in the 2007–2008 academic year.

Transitioning from Populating to Preserving to Publishing

As we developed our IR, we realized we were moving from a role of content manager to a role of publisher. Our first project with the honors program demonstrates this. In the past, honors projects were listed in OCLC but were only available through interlibrary loan. Now, the projects are born digital, "published" in the IR, and immediately visible to the world. We added to our IR by uploading staff articles and PowerPoint presentations such as our presentation at the SPARC Digital Repositories Conference in November 2008. A Macalester staff person was unable to find a publisher for his scholarly article. We welcomed the opportunity to upload the article on to Digital Commons. He now receives "fan mail" and about 50 downloads per month. He says of this successful venture, "It isn't *The Da Vinci Code*, but I'm happy with it."

We have several student peer-reviewed journals in our IR. The *Macalester Journal of Philosophy* was originally a print-based journal best known only within the Philosophy Department. The library director approached the faculty advisor about adding the journal to the IR, and it now has a digital presence and is available to all. The *Macalester Islam Journal* and *Studies in Mediterranean Antiquity and Classics* are new born-digital journals. In both cases, the faculty advisors brought their interest in publishing a digital journal to members of DAM.

We also paid to have back issues of college publications digitized and are uploading them to our IR. Additional journals and college publications we publish through our IR include the following:

- *Bildhaan: An International Journal of Somali Studies* (Institute for Global Citizenship)
- *Himalaya, the Journal of the Association for Nepal and Himalayan Studies*
- *LMW News* (Library)
- *Macalester Abroad: Research and Writing from Study Away* (Institute for Global Citizenship)
- *Macalester International*
- *Macalester Today*

In addition to our publications, we pay fees for faculty articles that are published in open access journals. We have added links on our repository pages that feature an author's addendum among other aids to further promote the cause of open access.

Where Are We Today?

We have traced the success of our IR not only through activity but also through statistics. Full-text download statistics appear on our main IR page and are updated daily. Through statistics we gain insights into the power of an IR. For example, a new student journal that was created this summer, containing only four selected essays from students who studied abroad, has already had 455 full-text downloads. Other interesting statistics from our IR include

- 398 papers uploaded to date,
- 75,292 full-text downloads since 2005, and
- 43,248 downloads in 2008 (as of 11/6/2008).

Figure 10-1 shows full-text downloads for each year of the repository's existence. The far right group shows only the past six months of downloads. If downloading continues at the same rate, we will surpass our annual 400 percent increase by May 2010. The "other" category includes our faculty Selected Works pages and staff papers.

Where Are We Headed?

We are adding more partners, publications, and policies. Current initiatives include the following:

Figure 10-1. Downloads from DigitalCommons@Macalester College

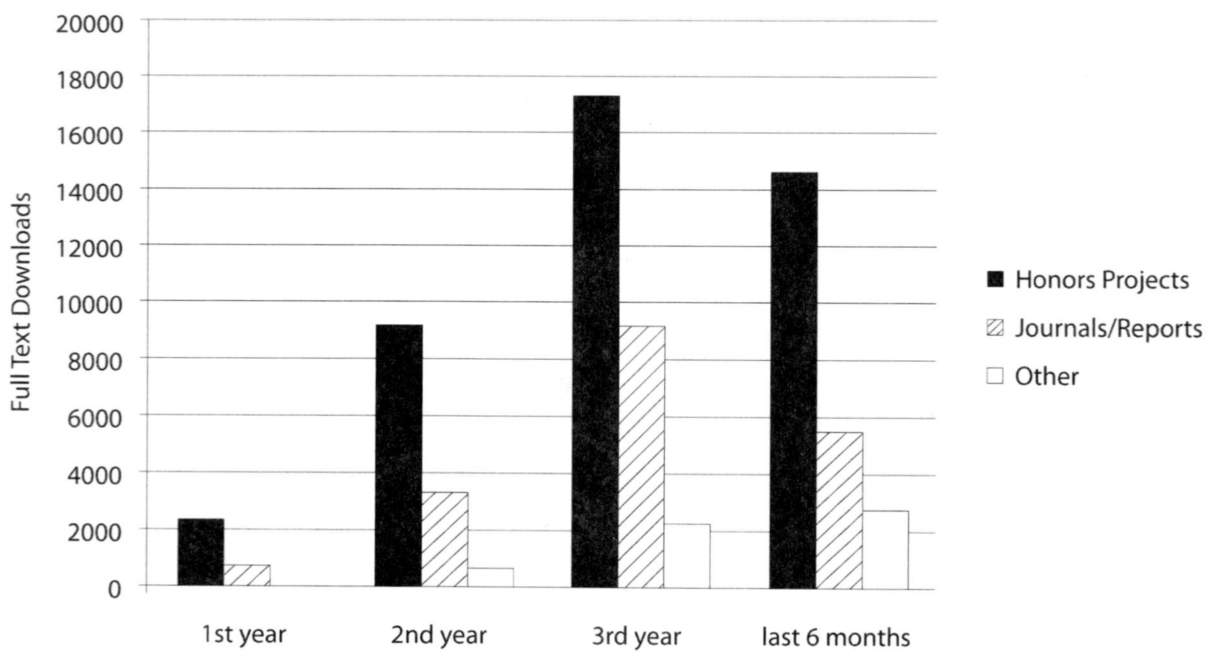

- Uploading all publications of the Institute for Global Citizenship. The Institute is a flagship organization at Macalester that offers an International Roundtable each Fall term. The Roundtable papers are always on reserve/electronic reserve, and the dean agreed to providing access through our IR. However, the dean was totally opposed to any other Institute material having open access, because he did not want people to think there was any such thing as a free lunch. He realized the value of the scholarship being available to the wider community, so one year later we were granted the opportunity to upload back and future issues of all publications originating in the Institute.
- Adding a physics journal, a new biogeography journal, an anthropology scholarly society journal, and a student peer-reviewed journal in American studies.
- Uploading two journals published elsewhere but edited by our faculty, who want to make sure their material is accessible to the broader academic community.
- Adding development documents, publicity pieces, and research data of the recently created Sustainability Office, which leads and promotes sustainability efforts on campus. The manager of the office had worked at another institution and all her work there was lost when she left; nothing was archived. She wanted to make sure this wouldn't happen at Macalester.
- Collaborating with the newly created campuswide Scholarly Publishing Committee. This committee functions as our editorial board and assists us in writing new policies to help us deal with requests we never imagined we would receive. For instance, a student requested his article be removed from one of our journals because a Google search on his name would retrieve the paper and reveal that he had gone to an expensive college in the United States. His family lives in a country that has a huge divide between the haves and have-nots, and he did not wish to run the risk of ill feelings toward his family. The committee has not ruled on this yet.

Road Map for Success, or Strategies That Worked for Us

We believe these are the pertinent points for those wishing to explore and implement an IR:

- Apply and leverage traditional skills in organizing and managing content.
- Collaborate with effective partners.
- Jump in and avoid "death by planning." We were planful, but it came to the point where we just said, "Damn the torpedoes, full speed ahead."

- Start with a project that meets a specific need and a specific audience.
- Engage students, because they are the future for scholarly publishing. Students understand the model; they are interested and engaged.
- Promote at every opportunity—involve *everyone.*
- Generate success with success—one enthusiastic department encourages others, one journal leads to the next, one idea sparks new initiatives and engenders new partners.

Conclusion

Implementing an IR is a rewarding experience. We successfully integrated our IR processes into our workflow and have continued to promote it and take advantage of a wide range of opportunities. It has not been easy, but the rewards have made it worth all the effort. Showcasing student publications has led to new opportunities and has demonstrated how the library can be an effective partner in publishing. The process of becoming a publisher takes time, energy, persistence, and constant communication. A contributor to our success, and an essential partner in our efforts, is our vendor, which provides excellent support. We continue to be approached by faculty with requests to start new publications, and the library is exploring collaborating with a faculty member to produce our first online "book-length" publication. We believe this effort will position us for future publishing developments that will further enhance our role as the gateway and comprehensive information center of Macalester College, as well as adding value to our institution.

IDEALS:
Shifting to a Service Focus at the University of Illinois

Sarah L. Shreeves

11

IN THIS CHAPTER:

- ✔ Introduction
- ✔ Brief History of IDEALS
- ✔ IDEALS' Scope, Policies, and Services
- ✔ Lessons Learned
- ✔ References

Introduction

IDEALS (Illinois Digital Environment for Access to Learning and Scholarship, online at www.ideals.illinois.edu) is the set of scholarly communication services and collections that use the institutional repository (IR) as infrastructure at the University of Illinois at Urbana–Champaign. IDEALS is a joint initiative of the University Library and the Campus Information Technology and Education Services (CITES), the central information technology (IT) unit on the Illinois campus. Since opening its doors in 2006, IDEALS has grown to include over 8,000 items (including published material, gray literature, presentations, data sets, student research, and blog posts) with representation from 60 percent of the colleges and schools on campus. IDEALS now sees approximately 1,400 downloads per day. While IDEALS was originally initiated as a traditional IR, that is, as a repository-centric infrastructure to collect, manage, provide access to, and preserve research produced on campus, the program is slowly and steadily shifting to provide a range of services to support scholarly communication activities in close collaboration with faculty, academic units, and students. This case study provides a brief history of IDEALS and an overview of IDEALS services, infrastructure, policies, and scope, and it discusses some of the services and projects under the scope of IDEALS and reflects on lessons learned.

Brief History of IDEALS

In mid-2004, the University Library and CITES proposed an IR service to the provost in a white paper titled "Illinois Digital Scholarship: Preserving and Accessing the Digital Past, Present and Future" (Grady, Mischo, and Sandore, 2004). The white paper focused on two issues: the growing complexity of the digital scholarly environment, particularly for preservation of the output of the academic enterprise, and the need for new models of digital scholarship. The IR would provide an essential infrastructure for the university to both preserve the output of the university and provide a way to influence the current scholarly communication system. The proposal was successful: the Office of the Provost provided six years of funding (approximately $700,000 total) to the University Library and CITES to get the IR established and off the ground with the expectation that it would be assessed at the completion of the six years and either incorporated into operational budgets as a standard campus service or phased out.

IDEALS thus started off with several advantages that many IRs do not have: high-level administrative support, dedicated resources over a relatively long period of time, and a collaborative partnership between two campus organizations. The funding allowed the library to hire two full-time staff members in late spring of 2005 to support the IR: a coordinator and a technical lead. A working group that included faculty, librarians, archivists, and CITES staff was also formed to provide guidance for IDEALS staff. One of the first decisions of this working group was the software to be used. DSpace was chosen over Eprints, Fedora, and Xythos (a commercial product) because it was open source, could be installed quickly, and had a relatively large and active user community in the United States. However, the group perceived a number of gaps in the software and identified areas that the technical lead could customize. This working group was also responsible for the establishment of policies (such as the collection policy, access restrictions, etc.). A subset of the working group, led by the Preservation Librarian, began to look at preservation issues.

Between June 2005 and April 2006, IDEALS staff focused on implementation and customization of the DSpace software, working with university counsel to establish the license agreement and intellectual property policies, document policies and procedures, plan for digital preservation activities, and perform preliminary outreach to librarians, faculty, and others. IDEALS opened its doors for deposits in April 2006; it ran in pilot mode until October 2007 when its technical infrastructure was moved from the University Library's servers into the CITES data center and it was designated a production-level service. As IDEALS transitioned from a project to a programmatic service (organizationally it sits under the Office of Information Technology Planning and Policy in the University Library), the working group was disbanded. The Preservation Working Group continues its work with a focus on meeting the requirements for a trustworthy repository using the "Trustworthy Repositories Audit and Certification: Criteria and Checklist" (RLG-NARA Digital Repository and Certification Task Force, 2007).

The development of the checklist was the responsibility of a joint task force between the Research Libraries Group and the National Archives and Records Administration. It has since been updated, and the revision is available at the Center for Research Libraries' Web site at **www.crl.edu/content.asp?l1=13&l2=58&l3=162&l4=91**.

Over the past three years we have heavily customized the DSpace software. Customizations include the additions of statistics that count number of downloads, community-level administrator functionality, ability to rearrange the steps in the deposit process, and an overnight process that converts certain types of file formats like Microsoft Word or Excel to a less platform-dependent file format like PDF or CSV for access purposes. The IDEALS technical lead, Tim Donohue, is one of 15 DSpace committers (DSpace developers who can commit code to the central DSpace code repository) worldwide, and most of these customizations have been made available to the DSpace community or have been added to the central DSpace code.

IDEALS' Scope, Policies, and Services

From the start IDEALS has had a clear scope in terms of the types of materials that could be deposited. IDEALS collects, manages, and preserves the research and scholarship produced at the University of Illinois as well as materials that reflect the intellectual environment of the university. Administrative records, standard curricular material, and digitized special collections except those that represent scholarship from the university fall outside of the collection development scope of IDEALS. "Materials that reflect the intellectual environment of the university" can include resources like journals that are produced at the university but contain articles from researchers outside of the institution and talks given by researchers from other institutions. Faculty, staff, and graduate students can deposit directly into IDEALS; a faculty member must sponsor undergraduate work. Current material in IDEALS ranges from faculty pre- and postprints, entire journal runs, data sets, technical reports, and working papers to video, audio, and a selection of student work. Like most DSpace installations, IDEALS is organized into communities and collections that tend to correspond to research and academic units on campus. Communities are established in consultation with the units and individuals involved and may be managed according to the needs of that unit or individual within the bounds of IDEALS' policies and procedures.

IDEALS has fairly standard policies and procedures in place. All IDEALS policies and procedures can be found at https://services.ideals.uiuc.edu/wiki. They are also archived within IDEALS itself. They are reviewed on an annual basis but also are updated more frequently as the need (generally in the form of a situation that we had not anticipated) arises. The policies that IDEALS staff refer to most frequently are outlined here:

- **Collection Policy:** The collection policy outlines the collection scope for IDEALS, as well as who can and cannot deposit into IDEALS. This policy is quite valuable in that it outlines the dimensions of the collection in IDEALS and has allowed IDEALS staff to say no to some material that is clearly outside its boundaries.
- **Intellectual Property Policy, including the license agreement:** The intellectual property policy and the nonexclusive distribution license for IDEALS was developed in collaboration with university counsel. Of special concern was what the depositor would warrant when depositing and, therefore, what the university was not taking responsibility for. For example, if a copyright dispute arises, IDEALS will withdraw the contested item

until resolution has been reached. IDEALS will not act to resolve the issue, however, as this is the responsibility of the depositor.

- **Digital Preservation Policy, Digital Preservation Support Policy, Service Level Definition, and Format Recommendations:** This set of policies and recommendations form the core of the digital preservation policies for IDEALS. The guiding principle behind IDEALS' preservation activities and commitment is that the service be explicit and open about what it can and cannot commit to in terms of long-term preservation. These policies and procedures were developed and honed after participation in the Digital Preservation Management Workshop (offered at Cornell at the time, but now offered through the Interuniversity Consortium for Political and Social Research [ICPSR] at the University of Michigan) and a continuing review of the "Trustworthy Repositories Audit and Certification: Criteria and Checklist" (RLG-NARA Digital Repository and Certification Task Force, 2007).
- **Access Restriction Policy:** Although the IDEALS program strongly prefers that materials deposited in IDEALS have no access restrictions placed on them, this policy outlines when and how access restrictions can be instituted. IDEALS' implementation of DSpace has been customized to allow a depositor to place an embargo or restrict access to a specific group during the deposit process.
- **Access and Use Policy:** While the policies described are aimed at the depositor audience, the Access and Use Policy is explicitly directed at end users of the material in IDEALS and covers issues such as accessibility, copyright, and IDEALS' commitment to open and reliable access to the research it contains.

Other policies include withdrawal, metadata, and community policies as well as frequently asked questions that support and augment the developed policies.

IDEALS offers or is developing the following services:

- **Bulk deposit:** Often a department or research center will have a large set of material to deposit with associated metadata in spreadsheets, databases, or citation management software like RefWorks. IDEALS staff will map the metadata into DSpace's internal format and import all of the files at once.
- **Mediated deposit:** In addition to bulk deposit, IDEALS staff will also deposit individual items on behalf of researchers; this often occurs particularly with researchers who are either too busy or too uncomfortable with the deposit interface.
- **Consulting on author rights:** IDEALS staff will consult with faculty and researchers on what may or may not be deposited based on publisher policies. This consultation includes writing to publishers to request permission for deposit as well as general

guidance on how to read copyright transfer agreements. In addition, IDEALS offers workshops throughout the semester for graduate students on author rights. Early in the establishment of IDEALS this set of services had been thought to be outside of the scope of IDEALS; it quickly became apparent, however, that this was a crucial service to provide.

- **Digitization services:** IDEALS works in collaboration with the Digital Content Creation unit in the University Library to provide digitization services for faculty and departments. This includes both individual and runs of items.
- **Consulting on data sets (pilot):** IDEALS does accept small- to medium-sized data sets and works with researchers to determine what other materials should be included with the data set(s) to make them interpretable and usable.
- **Analysis of faculty publication history (in development):** IDEALS is collaborating with staff at the University of Wisconsin–Madison in the Wendt Engineering Library and the University Library system on the development of BibApp. This software application allows an institution to gather the publication history of its faculty, present it in a variety of views, automatically perform a preliminary assessment of which publications may or may not go into a repository, and push those publications that can be deposited directly into a repository using standard protocols. Although BibApp is still in active development, it has the potential to be a useful and compelling "front door" to IDEALS or any IR.

An example of a data set in IDEALS can be found at **http://hdl.handle.net/2142/3524**.

For more information on BibApp, see **www.bibapp.org**.

In addition, the University Library is exploring collaboration opportunities to provide journal and conference proceeding publishing services (via Open Journal Systems or other means) under the umbrella of IDEALS.

Lessons Learned

As IDEALS passes into its third year, the lessons we learned may be useful to other organizations considering or implementing an IR. Perhaps the most significant lesson for the University Library and CITES was that the success of IDEALS would be predicated on it shifting from a repository-centric service to a program with a set of services for which the repository provided infrastructure but not its raison d'être. This change in perspective is not unique to the University of Illinois (Salo, 2009; Duranceau, 2009) but allowed the IDEALS program to reframe and expand its services in terms of the actual needs of faculty and researchers within the larger scholarly communication environment. An important outcome of this shift has been the slow but steady uptake by subject liaison librarians of the full range of IDEALS services as tools for collection development and dialogue with faculty and departments. IDEALS staff also offer general consulting on author rights and data curation even if the outcome of those conversations does not result in the deposit of items into the IDEALS repository but into a disciplinary, funder's, or even no repository. In addition, the workshops offered for graduate students on author rights do not tend to directly benefit the IDEALS repository but hopefully provide a foundation for decisions by future faculty members at other institutions. Although this shift in perspective may seem subtle, it has proven invaluable in allowing IDEALS to build a strong foundation for a range of scholarly communication services.

Other lessons learned include the following:

- *Do not rely on self-archiving by researchers.* Like most repositories, IDEALS was originally conceived with the idea that researchers would deposit their materials on their own. This was quickly discovered to not be the case, and IDEALS has since shifted to mediated deposit, bulk deposit, and automated identification of items for deposit. Also, as described previously, IDEALS focuses on far more than just the published literature; gray literature such as technical reports and working paper series are considered important parts of the scholarly record at the University of Illinois and are prime candidates for inclusion into the repository. Another "easy win" has been establishing an electronic thesis and dissertation program with the Graduate College.
- *Understanding the scholarly publishing and communication landscape of a discipline is critical to a fruitful discussion with a researcher in that discipline.* The discussion with an engineering faculty member about IDEALS services is different than that with a history faculty member because of disciplinary differences in the scholarly publishing landscape. For example, in the experience of IDEALS staff, humanities faculty tend to be more uncomfortable sharing preprints or nonauthoritative versions of their research than those faculty in the physical sciences. Knowledgeable subject liaison librarians can assist in having these conversations with researchers.
- *Eliminate bureaucracy.* In a default DSpace installation, a depositor has to ensure that she has been given submission rights to a specific collection before depositing. This generally means that a potential depositor has to contact the repository manager or the manager of their collection to get permissions; if the potential depositor does not have a collection already established, she then has to have one set up, which may, in turn, mean involving her colleagues and department to get agreement about policies, who may deposit, etc. This last process can take a very long time. As an example, there is one community in IDEALS that took approximately two years to establish because the organization, description, and community policies had to be vetted in the department's executive committee. Early on, IDEALS established an open collection called "UIUC Research and Scholarship" that was open for deposit to any faculty, graduate students, and

staff at the University of Illinois. Because IDEALS is linked up to the campus' authentication system, depositors never have to e-mail IDEALS staff if they want to deposit; they can simply log in and are automatically given permission to deposit. This collection, however, is perhaps the best evidence within IDEALS of the failure of self-archiving: it currently holds only 100 items that have been deposited without any type of mediation on behalf of the depositors.

- *Enable flexibility.* In addition to eliminating bureaucracy, it is crucial to be flexible so that the needs of faculty and researchers can be met. Flexibility within the IDEALS repository has been enabled programmatically by allowing departments, research centers, and others to manage their own communities and collections. Within the scope of the general IDEALS guidelines, communities can decide who deposits, what is deposited, and the structure of the communities. IDEALS also regularly reviews and updates its policies, services, and functionality in light of user needs and requests.
- *Work with nontraditional users.* One of the most successful and interesting collaborations for IDEALS has been that with the Ethnography of the University Initiative (EUI) and is focused on building an archive of student research on the university and surrounding community. This cross-campus program offers students the opportunity to conduct original ethnographic and archival research on their own institutions and to archive this research, including the data from the field studies, in IDEALS for future students (and others) to build upon. The University Library works with the faculty directors of the EUI to educate both faculty and students involved in the program about publishing, open access, and copyright. This is also an important example of a program where the repository provides critical infrastructure.
- *Use a variety of success metrics.* There is ongoing discussion in the repository community on how to assess the success of a repository. The expansion of IDEALS to include a variety of scholarly communication services has forced the consideration of a much broader range of assessment metrics than just the standard ones of number of items in the repository and number of downloads. This framework of assessment is still under development but includes percentage of departments whose faculty and graduate students have made some use of IDEALS services, understanding impact of workshops and other consulting services, tracking where citations to material in the repository appear (e.g., in Wikipedia, blogs, or tweets), and how material in the repository is used or reused.

Most critical to the success of IDEALS has been time, resources, and high-level administrative support. That the initiative was originally conceived with six years of dedicated funding allowed the program to experiment and to develop useful services. The timeline also recognized that much of the impetus behind IDEALS meant significant culture changes that would take a long time to occur. Dedicated resources allowed focused attention on services. The high-level administrative support—from the University Library, the Office of the CIO, and the Office of the Provost—helped to establish the credibility of the program in the eyes of faculty members, department chairs, and deans of colleges, as well as within the library itself. As stated earlier, that IDEALS had time, dedicated resources, and high-level administrative support does make the program atypical of where most IRs begin, but the hope is that this case study provides an illustrative example of what can be possible if these three things are in place.

References

Duranceau, Ellen Finnie. 2009. "The 'Wealth of Networks' and Institutional Repositories: MIT, DSpace, and the Future of the Scholarly Commons." *Library Trends* 57, no. 2: 262–279.

Grady, Michael, William Mischo, and Beth Sandore. 2004. "Illinois Digital Scholarship: Preserving and Accessing the Digital Past, Present and Future." A White Paper prepared jointly by the University of Illinois Library and CITES. University of Illinois at Urbana–Champaign. Available: http://hdl.handle.net/2142/3 (accessed January 19, 2009).

RLG-NARA Digital Repository and Certification Task Force. 2007. "Trustworthy Repositories Audit & Certification: Criteria and Checklist." Version 1.0, February 2007. OCLC & CRL. Available: www.crl.edu/PDF/trac.pdf (accessed January 19, 2009).

Salo, Dorothea. 2009. "Innkeeper at the Roach Motel." *Library Trends* 57, no. 2: 98–123.

Implementing an Institutional Repository:

The Process at Texas State University–San Marcos

Joan L. Heath and Todd C. Peters

12

IN THIS CHAPTER:

Beginnings

In 2004, librarians at Texas State University's Alkek Library began following the development of institutional repositories (IRs) at other academic libraries. A former chair of the library's faculty advisory committee also contacted the library director to discuss ways to increase faculty awareness of research projects at the university. He and two colleagues identified this need during their participation in a Teaching with Technology Institute, a campus-sponsored workshop offered to faculty each summer. These overlapping interests provided the impetus for Texas State's IR. In retrospect, the relationships built over time between faculty and librarians, and faculty members' perception of the library as a reliable, unbiased provider of information and research were also key to the partnership.

A team of librarians with expertise in areas associated with an IR was formed (library administration, computer information services, cataloging, collection development, and reference). Five faculty members from the Colleges of Business, Education, and Science agreed to serve as an advisory body.

IR Platforms

A significant portion of early discussions on the implementation of an IR concerned platforms. Many questions had to be answered, including basics such as what can the software do, what kind of hardware is required, what is involved in setting up the software, and how much ongoing maintenance is required? Team members looked at several sites that already had working IRs. They also looked at vendor Web sites and project Web sites for open source solutions.

The team discussed and compiled lists of features that were available and would be required and also those that were not absolutely necessary. They identified interoperability and migration as core requirements of any solution. Interoperability means the solution must not be an isolated system. Therefore, the chosen platform must be able to interface and share data easily with other information systems on campus, such as the integrated library system, and external collections of information such as Google Scholar. This required the solution selected must be able to provide metadata in standard formats for harvesters.

Because preservation is another core function of the IR, the ability to easily migrate data and objects out of the system was deemed essential. This ability is most certainly true when hosting with a vendor so that no risk is involved if the library chose to migrate to a local system in the future. Any solution would need to support standard metadata formats such as Dublin Core. Also, it must be able to accept objects in digital formats suitable for preservation such as PDF/A.

The team also discussed implementation issues. Major concerns included the cost of hardware and software, the time to install and customize the system, and the complexity of day-to-day administration of the system. Most of the open source solutions looked at were Linux-based systems. The library did not have a full-time Linux system administrator or programmer on staff. It became apparent that an experienced Linux programmer would be needed to implement any of the open source solutions. In addition, there would be the cost of hardware to run the software. And, it would take several months to install the hardware and software and customize the look and feel of the platform.

In 2004, when the team began looking at IRs, there were not many hosted solutions. The team had onsite demonstrations and conference calls with some of the vendors that were available. Digital Commons, then offered by ProQuest, now licensed directly through its developer, bepress (Berkeley Electronic Press), was one of the hosted options considered. The team ultimately decided this was the best solution. One of the most attractive features was the ability for the library to begin hosting the IR immediately. There would be minimal setup time required to customize the look and feel, and a Linux programmer would not be required to set up the system. A concern with this platform, however, was room for growth, because subscribers paid based on storage used. It was the expectation that if the Texas State IR became successful, it could be migrated to a locally hosted open source solution, such as DSpace, in the future.

Staffing

Since its inception, the team has continued to manage the IR (locally named eCommons), with minimal staffing changes. Management includes establishing policies and procedures, adding and maintaining content, holding meetings and presentations with segments of the campus community, and regularly publicizing eCommons. Initial role assignments included the following:

- Technical support—Computer Information Services Librarian
- Content development—Collection Development Librarian and Electronic Resources Librarian

- Metadata and content loading—Serials Cataloger/Library Webmaster
- Outreach—Reference/Faculty Outreach Librarian
- Administrative support—Library Director

A student assistant was assigned to the Serials Cataloger, who handles the majority of the workload, to add and maintain IR content. Consideration was given to assigning a student assistant to the Faculty Outreach Librarian, who researches copyright permissions, but the complexity of these issues has delayed this action. Other changes to the IR team include the following:

- The Serials Cataloger/Library Webmaster position was modified, replacing the Webmaster responsibilities with a 50 percent assignment as the eCommons Manager.
- The Special Collections Cataloger position was added to assist with issues related to theses and dissertations.
- The Metadata Librarian position was added to the team (this new staff person was responsible for cataloging e-books and evolving metadata issues).

Budget

Aside from staffing costs, which were minimal, the primary expense was for the software license. As mentioned previously, the library licensed software that would allow a quick start for the IR. Thinking more long term, two years ago the library also began contributing financially to the development of the Texas Digital Library with the intention of migrating to this statewide repository at a later date. Fortunately, the Alkek Library budget was growing at the time the IR was implemented. Establishing a digital collections platform was considered an initiative worth funding.

Policies and the Working IR

The library did not try to construct all the policies before implementing the IR. Rather, policies were developed as the IR developed. Policies developed at the beginning of the project involved the scope and direction of the IR. First it had to be decided what would go into the IR. The team examined the types of intellectual output of the university, looked at the types of information put into other repositories, and looked at other existing platforms for disseminating works both on and off campus.

A fundamental characteristic for material eligible for inclusion was that it be primarily scholarly in nature. This would restrict faculty-produced works such as syllabi, vitae, and notes. Material of an instructional nature could be placed on the existing course information system built with SAKAI.

The team decided that ultimately individual departments should be the final arbiter of what is scholarly in their respective fields. However, it was realized that it was unrealistic to expect enthusiastic universitywide participation by departments in a new project like the IR, so the library would need to use its best judgment in order to simplify the process of getting material into the IR. Therefore, faculty and staff would be allowed to self-submit to the repository, but items would be reviewed by a librarian prior to inclusion. Undergraduate works must have a sponsoring department before the library will include them.

Because preservation is one of the core functions of the IR, a policy on removal of items from the IR was developed from the outset. The policy states that the archive is intended to be permanent. However, it acknowledges there may be special cases where an item needs to be removed from public view or from the archive. It provides the opportunity for newer versions of an item to be uploaded alongside the original.

Copyright is another issue that creates much confusion for both librarians and faculty. The team agreed items would only be included that did not infringe on someone else's copyright. In order for faculty to self-submit, a deposit agreement was created requiring that submitters declare they were either the owner of the copyright for the work or had obtained the necessary permission for the work to be included in the repository. The library decided to actively assist authors with copyright issues. A librarian will search the various open publisher lists, such as Sherpa, or contact publishers on the author's behalf to obtain the necessary permissions.

The IR is still a developing initiative, and flexibility is called for in all aspects. At its inception the IR team limited content scope to scholarship. Since then exceptions have been made to add articles, even books about the university history, or an academic program history. While this may be a more subtle than dramatic change, the scope of IR content could change further as the library selectively digitizes materials from Special Collections and the University Archives and seeks to have a common platform for all digital collections.

IR Content

The first list of proposed content drafted by the IR team included theses and dissertations, an electronic journal published locally, Applied Research Projects for the Master's in Public Administration program, Research Enhancement Grant Final Reports (university-funded grants), and individual faculty publications.

Adding theses and dissertations has been a major undertaking because it involves a change in university policy requiring electronic submission. Discussions with the Graduate School and the Graduate Council led first to a policy calling for electronic submission on a voluntary basis. Library staff worked with the Graduate College to develop policies and modify forms to facilitate the inclusion of electronic versions of theses and dissertations into the archive. Existing forms for submitting paper copies of theses and dissertations to the library for binding were modified to include the option of including a CD-ROM with an electronic version of the document. Only the copy approved by the Graduate College can be included in the repository. Also, any changes or modification must be approved by the Graduate College.

This practice has been in place for over a year. Although it has resulted in a number of theses and dissertations being added to the IR, only a quarter of theses and dissertations completed have been added. Hopefully, by the beginning of the next academic year university policy will require electronic submission and inclusion in the IR (unless the Graduate College authorizes a delayed release due to publisher restrictions, a pending patent, etc.). Additionally, in Fall 2008, software developed by the Texas Digital Library to manage electronic thesis and dissertation review and IR ingestion using a common submission form was demonstrated. This software, called Vireo, is now available and will be implemented by Texas State in Spring 2010.

The locally published journal the team hoped to add became problematic because of the lack of Unicode support in the IR software for mathematic symbols. However, at a later date, another journal, the *Journal of Texas Music History*, was added. Hosting journals is a content area the team continues to pursue. Publication series of student works have proven to be highly successful. Applied Research Projects in Public Administration and Honor's Program theses are routinely added to the IR, and the College of Education may add a student research series. Another early series was the Final Reports of the Research Enhancement Grants. Although these reports are summaries of university-funded grants, the team hopes faculty will realize benefit from adding content to the IR leading to additional contributions. Another content area worth mining is the technical report series. The Computer Science Department began using eCommons to host their series several years ago. Most interesting has been the pattern developing from individual faculty members. It is difficult to know what triggers a faculty member's initial decision, but, after a work has been posted to the IR, faculty will often forward additional works or their vitae for copyright permissions research. This has occurred with faculty in biology, clinical laboratory research, English, philosophy, and political science, to name a few.

After several months of publicizing eCommons, several results became apparent. Although reaction to the IR was positive, faculty were not rushing to add their scholarship in large numbers. The team's collective outreach appeared to successfully establish the library in the role of managing an IR, and faculty were actively supportive for adding student work (e.g., theses, dissertations, honors papers, applied research projects), but getting faculty to take the next step to contribute themselves was much slower and a very individual matter.

Still holding firm to the belief that the fundamental purpose of the IR is appropriate and worthwhile, the team realized building up content would take time with gradual achievements. Faculty concerns about risk to commercial publishing, especially for those working toward tenure, remain an issue. Librarians continue to introduce the IR at New Faculty Orientation and promote it further in workshops designed for faculty. However, outreach is also focused on more established researchers, appealing to their interest in the broader access to their work offered by the IR, new exposure to works published in the past, and an opportunity to permanently preserve their work into the future.

Marketing

The importance (and challenge) of marketing the concept of the IR to the university community was apparent to the team from the start. The communication plan focused on three objectives: (1) defining the purpose and value of an IR to individual authors, academic departments, the university overall, and the public at large; (2) explaining how the IR works, including the scope of content and basic policies and procedures, emphasizing improved access through Internet search engines, ease of adding content, and support for addressing copyright issues; and (3) ensuring the library's long-term commitment to access and preservation of IR content.

The team targeted specific audiences using a variety of approaches:

- Vice President for Information Technology (organizationally the library reports to the VPIT)
- Introduction/Information Session for the library staff
- Established a brand for the IR (eCommons) used in publications, Web site, etc.
- Presentation to the Faculty Senate
- Presentation to the Library Committee
- Presentation to the Dean's Council
- Individual meetings with deans and chairs
- Meetings with college councils
- Supporting communication from the Provost (sent to all faculty)
- Articles in the library's newsletter, *Bookmarks*
- *Library Beat* articles (a weekly library column in the university newspaper)
- Individual conversations with faculty members
- Presentation to Graduate Council
- E-mail distributions to faculty
- Various faculty workshops (Teaching with Technology, Showcasing Your Research, and Demystifying Publishing)

Increasing and Assessing Use

Texas State knew the importance of selecting a platform compatible with the Open Archives Initiatives Protocol for Metadata Harvesting (OAI-PMH). This allows metadata to be regularly harvested and made available in search engines such as OAIster. As it turns out, having the metadata harvested by Google has proved to be the primary mechanism of directing users to content in the IR.

Texas State has seen increased interest in the IR from faculty resulting from a positive feedback cycle. Authors are delighted when they begin receiving automatic e-mails indicating the number of hits/downloads of their work in the IR. Authors might initially only upload a few works to the repository but, upon seeing the usage results, express interest in including more from their bibliography.

Although it is a slow process, individual successes perhaps do the most to legitimize the IR. Thanks to an early faculty adopter, all of the Applied Research Projects for the Master's in Public Administration (including retrospective reports) have been added to eCommons. The faculty member in charge of this program went on to add all of her own work and has become one of our strongest champions at the university. There are numerous examples of unanticipated benefits to students after their work is added to the IR, such as using examples of their writing for job interviews, one student being contacted to serve on a national panel after his paper was discovered online, and another student invited to meet with a city council resulting from her work in the IR. The impact this has on the next generation of researchers is significant.

Our next strategy is to interview selected faculty about publication and research in their particular discipline. We expect to benefit not only with more content for the IR but also with a better understanding of their research and information needs.

We will continue to make it easy for the contributor. As part of the university's upcoming SACS reaccreditation, faculty vitae are being updated. With this information in hand, we plan to contact selected faculty and offer to research copyright permissions for IR inclusion.

Next Steps

Shortly after Texas State launched its IR, the Texas Digital Library (TDL) was created as a multi-university consortium to provide digital infrastructure support for scholarly communication for institutions of higher education in the state of Texas. Among the goals of the TDL is to have a centralized digital repository and to create a statewide preservation network for storing digital objects. Texas State joined the TDL consortium to further expand the reach of scholarly publications. TDL uses DSpace to provide hosting services to member institutions. Texas State is now exporting metadata into the TDL DSpace repository, although the process has not been straightforward and has required scripting and using XSLT transformations to modify the XML coding to conform to the TDL schema. Currently the library is evaluating the addition of a Linux programmer/analyst staff position to help with migration issues to TDL. A likely future direction for Texas State when TDL achieves a mature platform is to mirror local digital objects as well as metadata into TDL. This will probably steer the Texas State IR toward migration to DSpace, because real-time mirroring would be difficult, if not impossible, with a vendor-hosted system.

Enabling Innovation from Day One:

The Institutional Repository at the University of New Mexico

13

Johann van Reenen

IN THIS CHAPTER:

Introduction

Institutional repositories (IRs) raise questions about content: what recruitment techniques are successful, what types should be collected, what if any access restrictions will there be, and, ultimately, will it be useful and will it be used? This case study focuses on decisions for the new IR manager in two areas: whether to implement an IR locally or as part of a consortium; and setting rules, roles, and guidelines for who can submit and what can be submitted. The latter leads unavoidably to issues of content recruitment and the broader discussion of whether the IR should be restricted to only postprints of peer-reviewed articles or if it should support alternative and experimental content types and publishing.

These decisions will affect institutions with limited resources (financial and personnel) more in the first instance but will probably have no effect on the latter. Both decisions will affect the impact of your IR at different levels. I hope the experiences that informed our decisions will be helpful for the first-time IR manager and start-up planning or working groups.

Working Together or Alone

No project actually ever is or should be a one-person effort. However, starting up a local IR is generally the job of one or two persons (and perhaps a committee!) with no other support than access to a user group or expertise at another organization. Often it is a rather lonely job.

At the University of New Mexico (UNM) Libraries we were fortunate to be a member of the *Alliance for Information Science & Technology Innovation* (AISTI; www.aisti.org) whose members decided to study existing IRs and create a test instance for all members to explore. A study was commissioned in 2003 to report on the types of software available, the functionality these offered, costs, and the ease of implementation. In 2004 an instance of the chosen software (DSpace) was installed at the Research Library of the Los Alamos National Laboratories. The idea was that this would be a proof-of-concept and then individual implementations at each organization would follow. This experiment led to a rather long period of discussion and indecision about the merits of a consortial IR. A decision had to be made whether to offer consortial IR services to members, to others thinking of starting their own, support a subject specific IR for AISTI on topics in Information Science and Innovation, or disband the IR and start individual IRs depending on interest at our parent organizations. These discussions are still occurring at various levels.

In a similar setting, an IR taskforce of the *Greater Western Library Alliance* (GWLA, 2007–2008) was asked to explore the interest of members in starting a consortial IR. Although this was not part of our official survey, it was interesting to note that the reasons for this have changed since discussions in the early 2000s. Some had experience with running an IR but found it expensive or too complex (the latter was usually a function of the software chosen). Others explored commercial options such as bepress' IR product *Digital Commons*, which was launched in 2004. Other respondents were more interested in a support group for new IRs.

The related concept of subject or centralized repositories, also called CRs, is worth examining. It is likely to come up in discussions with faculty, especially those in fields such as biomedicine that have centralized repositories. There was already a discussion about this among American scientists in the early stages of IR development (Harnad, 2005), which continues on today (Harnad, 2008). It is of particular interest in Europe and Britain where repository mandates are more common.

For Harnad (2005), the answer is clear:

> The dilemma has a simple, optimal and universal solution, with many, many good reasons supporting it: Direct deposit should be in each researcher's own institution's IR. SRs and CRs can harvest from IRs. That's what the OAI protocol is for. Institutions are the (distributed) research providers. They are the ones with the direct stake in the record-keeping and showcasing of their own research output, in maximizing its accessibility, visibility, usage and impact, and in assessing and rewarding its research performance. Institutions are also in the position to mandate that their own research output be deposited in their own IR; funder mandates can reinforce that, and can benefit from institutional monitoring and oversight (as long as funders too mandate institutional deposit and central harvesting, rather than direct central deposit).

This may be a sufficient (and brief!) answer to this question should it arise. However, it is good to follow the constantly emerging issues in open access mandates to ensure that the IR team can respond with current thinking to researchers' concerns. The bottom line: good metadata results in successful harvesting between repositories and/or subject portals, which in turn ensures good dissemination and correct citation, all issues of major concern for scientists.

During the test of the AISTI joint repository it became clear that participants have very different expectations about what an IR can do for their organization. Some see it as a way to ensure open access to peer-reviewed published articles and thus as an effort to combat the rising cost of subscriptions.

Others see it as a mechanism to educate researchers, graduate students, and faculty on the benefits of open access, individual publishing rights management, and the broader dissemination of their research output and that of the organization at large. Still others see it as an opportunity to provide all the benefits described but also experiment with new ways of publishing all the useful formalized information created by the academic enterprise, such as planning documents, white papers, and student publications.

This divided vision of what a consortial IR should provide was further complicated by branding issues. However, the main deal breaker was who and how such an IR would be administered and what a fair funding model would be. We decided to disband the test IR instance in favor of local IRs. Eventually only two of the ten participants developed their own local IR over the following two years.

UNM started its IR immediately after the consortial test. One of the first major decisions was the scope of the IR. UNM has a main campus, a law campus, a medical campus, and four branch campuses, all with their own independent library systems. Should each have its own instance of DSpace? The planning group decided to create an IR for the main campus initially. Then we would proselytize for it at our annual scholarly publishing symposium and when visiting the other campus library systems. The provost at the time was interested enough to allow the group to update him regularly as the implementation progressed. By the time we needed to make a firm decision, faculty from the other campus locations had found the IR and were depositing items independently! We could thus make a compelling argument for a single UNM DSpace instance serving all stakeholders. Concurrent to this process we established the Institutional Repository Working Group (IRWG) to which library representatives from all sites were invited.

Content Policy Development: Documenting the Work of the Academy

The IRWG, consisting of members from UNM's Law Library, the Health Sciences Library and Informatics Center, and the University Libraries, created a subgroup to develop a philosophy, and the practices flowing from that, for the types of communities, collections, and content that would be encouraged for the UNM's IR.

Early in the IR movement (2003), Smith et al. of the DSpace working group decided that the aim of their IR would be to capture and preserve all types of scholarship created by faculty, not only research articles but also a wide range of content types including gray literature, theses, cultural materials, scientific data sets, institutional records, and educational materials. At UNM we decided that this philosophy would inform our work. We wanted to capture works, that is, digital objects of all kinds, that represent every step in the research to discovery to teaching cycle. This could include grant information, minutes of important and potentially historic meetings, white papers, reports (both technical and progress), graduate student works, laboratory notes, and anything else that results from academic work. Our group struggled with the potential "watering down" of the content should it be perceived to have minimal collections of peer-reviewed postprints. The literature then and now, as discussed earlier, indicated that an IR based on peer-reviewed postprints would have at best a slow uptake; this may, over time, discourage the IR movement and the enthusiasm of submitters. We hoped that an eclectic mix of materials that needed archiving but for which there was no system in place to do so, including material that is useful in graduate work, class preparation, and pre-research materials, would draw submitters for the utility the IR offers and begin to educate them on the value of capturing the diversity of intellectual output at UNM. A smaller group of us believed that more complexity is a good thing and could lead to unexpected innovation (van Reenen, 2006). We reviewed the IR policies developed at MIT for their historic DSpace implementation and found that most of these fit our philosophy and hopes.

UNM's IR Policies

Information about UNM's IR rules and conventions are documented at **https://repository.unm.edu/dspace/handle/1928/287/browse-title**.

As mentioned, a decision was made at UNM to implement only one instance of DSpace as the IR for the Albuquerque campus and all the branch campuses. The policies outlined in this section took this into account; once again pointing to less rather than more control.

Community Guidelines

The UNM IR is a partnership among UNM communities. The UNM IR's content consists of collections produced by UNM communities, which are managed, preserved, and distributed through the UNM. Some of the collections will be subject to institutional guidelines set by UNM Libraries and by the Health Sciences Library and Informatics Center. As in all partnerships, it is important that all stakeholders understand and agree to the policies, guidelines, and procedures required to build the repository.

These guidelines were soon tested in the area of items "produced by UNM communities." UNM is known as the "University for the Americas" based on its long association with Latin American universities and hemispheric research efforts, especially in the areas of education, public policy, health care, and economic and social development. Many submitters had materials from partners in these countries, from Latin American organizations such as the *Ibero-American Science and Technology Education Consortium* headquartered at UNM, or resulting from joint projects. Should IRWG insist on UNM-based and developed items only? This seems shortsighted and not representative of the university's larger role in the international academy. So, within a relatively short time, we modified the guidelines to include communities, collections, and materials related to UNM's broad reach. Some of the most interesting collections come from this extended reach, as will be discussed.

What Is a UNM IR Community?

An IR "community" is an administrative unit at UNM that produces research, has a defined leader, has long-term stability, and can assume responsibility for setting community policies. Each community must be able to assign a coordinator who can work with UNM librarians. Groups wishing to establish a community that do not fall into this definition will be considered on a case-by-case basis. Individuals may not submit items without belonging to an established community in UNM's IR.

What Are a UNM IR Community's Responsibilities?

A community agrees to

- arrange for submission and description of content in consultation with the community's assigned librarian,
- make decisions about community and collection definitions in consultation with the community's assigned librarian,
- notify the assigned librarian of organizational changes affecting submissions,
- reply to annual reconfirmation requests of community information,
- understand and observe policies relevant to UNM's IR and educate community submitters regarding these policies,
- clear copyright for items submitted when the copyright owner is other than the author(s) or UNM, and
- decide upon a submission workflow for each collection.

What Are a UNM IR Community's Rights?

The community retains the right to

- decide policy regarding content to be submitted (within UNM IR Content Guidelines),
- decide who may submit content within the community,
- limit access to content at the item level either to UNM only or to specific individuals or groups,
- receive a copy of submitted content upon request,
- remove items and collections (as outlined in the Withdrawal Policy),
- approve addition of or elimination of subcommunities, and
- customize interfaces to community content.

What Are the IR's Responsibilities?

The UNM IR facility agrees to

- retain and maintain content submitted;
- distribute content according to community decisions (to UNM minimally, unless prior approval is granted by the IRWG Policy Committee);
- preserve content using accepted preservation techniques;
- provide access to UNM IR research;
- notify communities of significant changes to content, e.g., format migration; and
- if UNM Libraries ceases to support UNM's IR, it will return collections to existing communities and transfer to UNM Archives collections of communities that have ceased to exist.

What Are the IR's Rights?

The UNM IR facility retains the right to

- redistribute, sell, or amend metadata for items in the IR;
- refuse or deaccession items or collections under certain circumstances as outlined in the Withdrawal Policy;
- renegotiate terms of original agreement with communities;
- perform appraisal for long-term archiving when communities cease to exist or within 30 years of the creation of a collection;
- move collections to reflect current understanding between UNM's IR and communities;
- migrate items if format is in danger of obsolescence;
- set quotas (size of files, number of items) to determine what constitutes free service and after which point to charge a fee; and
- charge fee for activities requiring extensive centralized support from DSpaceUNM (e.g., large amount of deaccessioning).

What Are UNM's Responsibilities?

The UNM IR facility is expected to

- set policy at the institute level regarding issues that affect UNM IR, e.g., copyright rules, thesis requirements; and
- support functions mandated by existing policies.

Purposing the IR to Archive the Complete Research Cycle

> The research production cycle has three components: the conduct of the research itself (R), the data (D), and the peer-reviewed publication (P) of the findings. Open Access (OA) means free online access to the publications (P-OA), but OA can also be extended to the data (D-OA). (Brody et al., 2007)

Example 1. IDEC: Imagery Data Extraction Collaborative

Scientific fields of study such as microbiology, astrobiology, and cave and karst sciences contain large collections of images (in our case scanning electron micrographs [SEMs]) and their associated biological, physiochemical, and geological data sets. The vast majority of these images are never shared or examined by more than a handful of scientists. IDEC (http://idec.aisti.org) consists of an integration of three open source tools: Drupal, Gallery, and UNM's DSpace-based IR. Drupal is an open source content management system, and Gallery is an open source image management system that can be integrated directly into Drupal. A commenting function was implemented in UNM DSpace to allow viewers to provide their insights from viewing the images (Figure 13-1). All three tools are relatively easy to install and configure and are widely used globally. IR staff and the research group decided to test using this configuration as a proof-of-concept for developing our broader collaborative workspaces for knowledge discovery with Weblogs, forums, feeds, and image functionality enabled.

Figure 13-2 shows the entry page for the IDEC Portal; on the lower right are examples of forum topics with their respective albums of SEM images. From here, users can click on the thumbnails to view the images in the album in a larger format. Title, date created, owner, and number of images of each album are displayed below the thumbnail. Comments

Figure 13-1. UNM DSpace Entry Page to the Scanning Electron Micrograph Collection

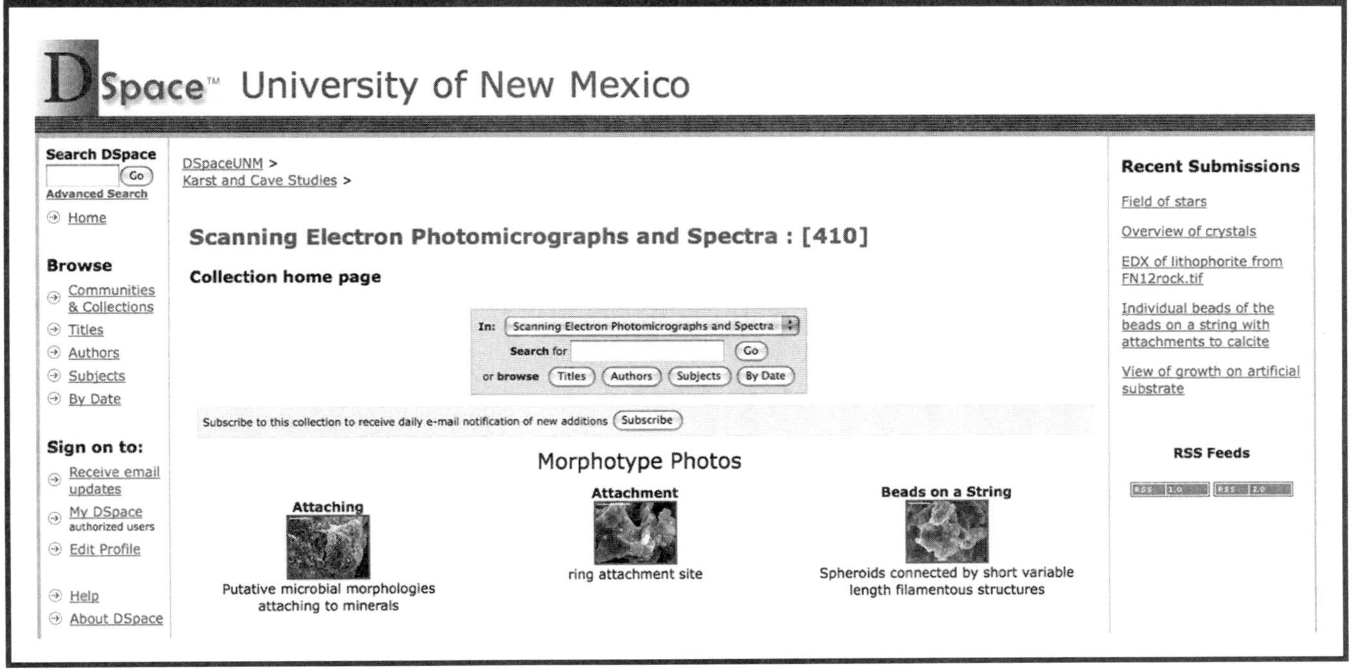

Figure 13-2. The IDEC Web Site with the Image Gallery

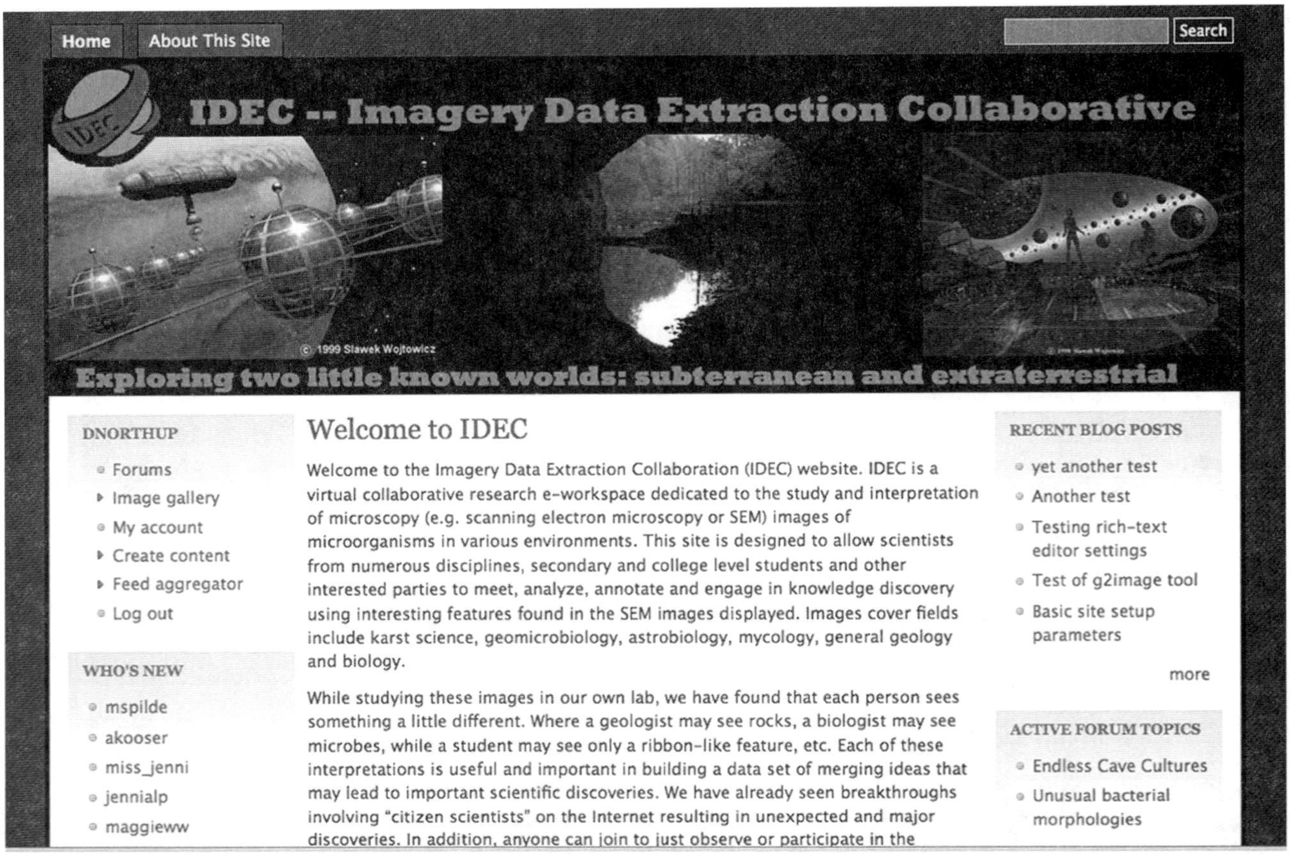

appear in real time below the images. The comments in the IR are provided as a searchable table.

We continue exploring ways to increase collaborative efforts among researchers. Participating in IDEC is often an additional activity for them and, as others have found (e.g., Seddon, Skinner, and Postlethwaite, 2008), sustained engagement in online communities is a challenge that requires ever more elegant technological enabling.

Example 2. The Nepal Study Center

UNM's Nepal Study Center (http://nepalstudycenter.unm.edu/index.htm) organized their Web site around a set of collections in the IR, publishing two new journals, *Himalayan Journal of Development and Democracy* and the *Liberal Democracy Nepal Bulletin*, and an archive of unique *Himalayan Research Papers* based on digital objects in the IR. The journals' Web sites in combination with the content of each issue in IR collections provide an extremely affordable e-journal publishing system managed by a graduate student for less than $3,000 per year.

Example 3. The Latin American Social Medicine Collection

The Latin American Social Medicine (LASM) collection (https://repository.unm.edu/dspace/handle/1928/3441) is one of the products of UNM's grant-funded *Latin American Knowledge Harvester* (http://retanet.unm.edu/lakh/en/index.html). It consists of three collections of structured abstracts in Spanish, Portuguese, and English in a highly developed field in Latin America, social medicine, that is just now emerging in the United States and reemerging in Europe. The IR challenge was to iterate the digital objects in each language version in a way that links the three versions together.

LASM is one of the collections that are harvested by a harvesting-only instance of DSpace at UNM (http://lakh.unm.edu). Others include metadata from IR collections in Ecuador, Mexico, Venezuela, and Brazil, some of which were established with the help of the UNM IR group using DSpace instances delivered via VMware (Virtual Machine Ware) to our grant partners.

Example 4. Collections from the Law School

UNM's Law School Library has utilized the UNM IR to its fullest to archive important and unique collections that require public accessibility. These include Governor Richardson's Task Force on Ethics Reform (2006); collections from the Indian Law Program, such as the *Sandia Pueblo Mountain Claim's* unique collections of U.S. District Court and Court of Appeals Case Documents; the recently started electronic version of the *New Mexico Law Review*; and a series of collections on the *Western Water Policy Review Advisory Commission's* work.

The UNM IR also houses electronic theses and dissertations, the minutes from the university's Board of Regents, documents from the Office of the President and the Office of the Vice-President for Research, the weekly Bulletins of the Anderson Schools of Management, Faculty Senate minutes, an e-book and various e-conference proceedings, professional reports completed by the Water Resources Program, additional data elements and sets for published print monographs, student works, technical reports, the University Libraries' disaster recovery archives from two floods and a major fire, and more.

Conclusion

As early adopters of open access systems and a universitywide IR, we have benefited from an experimental approach to content recruitment. This approach has allowed the IR to be used in compelling research proposals, to document the university's activities from research to administrative history, and augmented or enhanced traditional publishing. This is, however, not enough.

There are two models for Open Access: Gold and Green. Gold refers to journals that are Open Access, and that allow free access to their content to the entire world. PLoS Biology (**http://www.plosbiology.org/**) may be the most famous example of a Gold journal. Green refers to content posted in institutional repositories, usually but not exclusively applied to journal articles. The content may appear in any traditional journal, but (provided the publisher allows it) is also posted in the author's IR.

Our weakest link is the small number of peer-reviewed postprints of UNM faculty, the most important intellectual outcomes of our enterprise. We believe that the IR has reached many faculty in inadvertent ways; given this and their level of awareness, it is time for us to embark on a concerted effort to obtain copyright permissions for faculty articles published in "Green" and "Gold" journals.

Our approach will focus on the role of the subject librarians within their target departments. Faculty have the right *intent* but not the *time*. This is the area where we hope to find innovative automated systems to load articles and metadata in the future.

References

Brody, T., L. Carr, Y. Gingras, C. Hajjem, S. Harnad, and A. Swan. 2007. "Incentivizing the Open Access Research Web: Publication-Archiving, Data-Archiving and Scientometrics." *CTWatch Quarterly* 3, no. 3. Available: http://eprints.ecs.soton.ac.uk/14418/1/ctwatch.html#3 (accessed June 5, 2008).

Harnad, Stevan. 2005. "Central Versus Institutional Self-Archiving." E-mail to American Scientist Open Access Forum, May 9. Available: http://users.ecs.soton.ac.uk/harnad/Hypermail/Amsci/4475.html (accessed June 5, 2008).

Harnad, Stevan. 2008. "Institutional Repositories vs. Subject/Central Repositories. Open Access Archivangelism." Available: http://openaccess.eprints.org/index.php?/archives/414-Institutional-Repositories-vs.-Subject-Central-Repositories.html (accessed June 7, 2008).

Seddon, Kathy, Nigel C. Skinner, and Keith C Postlethwaite. 2008. "Creating a Model to Examine Motivation for Sustained Engagement in Online Communities." *Education & Information Technologies* 13, no. 1: 17–34.

van Reenen, Johann. 2006. "Open Access and Connectedness: Stimulating Unexpected Innovation through the Use of Institutional Open Archives." *Ciência da Informação* 35, no. 2: 17–26.

DigitalCommons@ University of Nebraska–Lincoln

14

Paul Royster

IN THIS CHAPTER:

Introduction

The institutional repository (IR) at the University of Nebraska–Lincoln (UNL) began operation in April 2005. The decision to implement an IR was made by the Dean of Libraries, Dr. Joan Giesecke, in 2004. After a study of the available platforms, the library selected the Digital Commons software developed by Berkeley Electronic Press (bepress) of California and (at that time) marketed and licensed through ProQuest of Ann Arbor, Michigan. The perceived advantages of this system were (1) its out-of-the-box functionality; (2) its single-price arrangement for software, server space, and ongoing support; and (3) its offering by a known vendor with whom the library had an ongoing relationship. Policies, rationale, and mission statements were adopted wholesale from existing models as suggested by the bepress developers.

The IR (http://digitalcommons.unl.edu) was initially stocked with the complete set of UNL PhD dissertations since 1955, which UNL contracted with ProQuest to digitize and mount on the site. These were digitized from microfilm copies held at ProQuest/UMI and mounted as page-image PDF files, with most document files running from 10 to 20 MB. By contract with ProQuest, full-text access to this content is free for UNL users; non-UNL users have free abstracts and 24-page previews, with electronic copies available for purchase for about $40. Approximately 9,400 of these dissertations went online in April 2004 and were the only content in the IR for the first three months. About 1,400 have been added since, representing new degrees awarded and also extending the coverage back to the 1890s, when the first PhDs were granted at UNL.

The staff consisted of one full-time librarian (this author), holding the title of Coordinator for Scholarly Communications, who began in June 2005 and was hired specifically to manage and recruit content for the new IR. I had no previous library experience but did have a background of 25 years in scholarly publishing that included editorial, production, and copyright experience. At that time, I had been on the UNL campus about two and a half years with the English Department and the university press, so I had some faculty contacts and a general sense of the university's organization and its research strengths. The position I filled was created by the retirement of a longtime employee with collection development responsibilities, which were mostly shifted elsewhere. I reported directly to the dean; I had no staff and no steering committee—just an office, a computer, access to the library's resources, a great deal of independence, and a mandate to discover and do what was necessary to make the IR "successful." Just what "success" meant wasn't clear, but I set a goal for the first year of 1,500 articles—which was based on one article for each member of the UNL faculty.

Many members of the library faculty and staff were extremely helpful, offering materials, contacts, and advice and helping spread news of the program across campus, especially when they saw an opening that might prove fruitful. Associate Dean Beth McNeil introduced me to Stephen Vantassel and the Internet Center for Wildlife Damage Control, who have since contributed over 4,000 articles; Technical Services Librarian Sue Ann Gardner connected me with Scott Gardner, who has contributed both the *Online Dictionary of Invertebrate Zoology* and an extensive backfile of the *Journal of Parasitology*; and Mary Bolin not only contributed but also uploaded the backfiles of *Library Philosophy and Practice*. For my part, I followed up every lead and never said "No, we can't (or don't) do that."

I began by visiting the Web sites of UNL's many departments, schools, colleges, programs, centers, and institutes and by creating "communities" and "series" within the repository to hold the content I aimed to recruit. I organized the repository's collection alphabetically by subject (agronomy, biological sciences, chemical engineering, etc.) rather than by name (Institute for, Center for, Department of, etc.) or by organizational structure. Like any institution that has existed for 150 years, UNL has grown by accretion as much as by plan: it has two separate entomology departments, at least three departments of computer science, two centers for materials science, etc. After about six weeks, I had built a large (but mostly empty) repository with hundreds of community and series pages, each appropriately titled, linked to the Web page of the academic unit it was intended for, and marked with an appropriate graphic to help distinguish one from another.

In the intervals, I uploaded my own papers (about a half-dozen) and developed a set of Microsoft Word templates designed to provide improved onscreen display of the manuscripts that faculty would ultimately be depositing. (These templates have had relatively little impact and almost no use, but they were an attempt to address the translation of 8.5" × 11" vertical sheets of paper to a horizontal computer screen with a 4:3 aspect ratio.) School was not yet in session, so I called on what few faculty I knew and could find and offered to upload their eligible papers for them. I did this because I needed (1) something to do and (2) some content to show as examples when I began to make the rounds of department meetings with a recruitment pitch.

When the fall semester began in August, I began to seek appointments with department chairs and invitations to faculty meetings, to which I went armed with handouts and a PowerPoint presentation on the rationale of IRs, the benefits of online open access, and the ease of self-archiving. The faculty were generally polite and attentive and seemed interested, but the response rate was well under 5 percent—I got an average of about one inquiry per department, and only about half the inquiries produced any deposited content.

But meanwhile, other avenues were turning out to be much more productive. On a visit to the Nebraska State Museum's Parasitology Laboratory, I discovered that the director had a large "dictionary of invertebrate zoology" manuscript that had been peer-reviewed and contracted by the University of California Press but subsequently cancelled for financial reasons. He was struggling to publish it online on the museum's own Web site but had so far only managed to get partway through the As. At my persistent urging he agreed to let me have a go at it and several days later sent me the text in 99 WordPerfect files, which I concatenated and began to copyedit, design, and typeset. After about two and a half weeks (and roughly 25,000 clicks), we published it in PDF format as *Online Dictionary of Invertebrate Zoology* (http://digitalcommons.unl.edu/onlinedictinvertzoology), and the response was astounding. Coauthors Armand Maggenti and Scott Gardner were well-connected in their field, and the work had long been anticipated. By its second week online it was accounting for 40 percent of the IR's traffic, and it remains our most-downloaded work. Spending almost three weeks full-time on a single document seemed somewhat counterproductive at the time, but the dean was supportive and, as it turned out, perspicacious. We did get some additional documents out of it and made for improved searching and downloading as well by splitting out letters as separate files.

Around the same time, I first met with Stephen Vantassel, Webmaster for the Internet Center for Wildlife Damage Control—a multi-institutional (Cornell, Clemson, Utah State, and UNL) project that was engaged in digitizing "all" the conference proceedings in their field going back to the early 1960s. The problem was that they lacked a good platform for hosting this content; mounting it on their Web site required labor-intensive HTML coding and constant redesigns and revisions of their Web pages and created server space issues. We had the platform, and they had the content and funding to pay for digitizing more; it was a great and lucky match. They would furnish book-length RTF or PDF files, and I would split them into individual articles and post them to the various series created within their IR community. This connection has so far supplied more than 4,000 articles, about 20 percent of our total content.

Not everything worked out so well. My hopes of harvesting the Computer Science Department's online archive of technical reports and gray literature came to naught when they decided to write a robot program to automatically transfer all existing and new works; the program never got written, and their online archive has since disappeared in a Web site redesign. The Honors College raised my hopes of collecting 800–1,000 undergraduate honors projects annually, but this too has yet to come to pass.

Still, by the middle of the fall semester I was encouraged to find that the monthly downloads of the several hundred open access articles I had managed to recruit were already exceeding the downloads from the 9,400 toll-access dissertations. Nonetheless, I was dissatisfied with the rate of uptake among the faculty, so toward the end of the first semester I began offering "for a limited time only" to gather, clear permissions, and upload all the eligible articles for anyone who would send me a vita or a publication list. This did improve the response rate from about 5 percent to around 10 to 15 percent, which was encouraging and did much to keep me busier.

Toward the end of the spring semester of 2006, I met with a group of professors from the Department of Physics and Astronomy and boldly made them the same offer. One said, "Do you want everything?" "Absolutely! Everything." I replied. I did not realize then what I have come to know since: (1) physics has a tradition and wide acceptance of the practice of online archiving, and (2) physicists publish a ton of articles. About ten members of the department sent me their publication lists; the shortest had 150 articles, the longest more than 400. Fortunately, the major physics journal publishers have very favorable archiving policies, so most of these several thousand articles were eligible for posting as publisher's PDFs. But I was still distraught over how to deliver on the promises I had so rashly made.

The dean, however, came up with a modest work-study budget, and when school began the next August a student was hired. I began gathering the postable physics articles for the student to upload, and in about ten weeks we had worked through the entire backlog. So I went back to the physics department and recruited some more faculty, who were impressed (and perhaps a bit envious) that their colleagues had all this content online and were getting monthly reports showing how often it was being downloaded.

This second year I began to notice that the numbers of downloads were spiraling—each month's usage was triple that of the same month from the previous year; and this increase continued through the third year. Now, in our fourth year, it seems to have slowed, and we are merely doubling the downloads from 12 months ago.

To date, I would estimate that our student worker has uploaded at least 12,000 of the roughly 20,000 articles in the repository, whose application and efficiency have created another kind of challenge: I now have to find 30 to 50 postable articles a day just to provide enough work. This has spurred me to develop new strategies for recruiting or finding potential content:

- We mined the scholarly and research publications coming from within the university, such as the *Nebraska Beef Cattle Reports, Nebraska Swine Reports, Cornhusker Economics, Great Plains Research, Nebraska Studies in Language and Literature,* and *Mid-West Quarterly.*
- We took advantage of the federal employee exception to the copyright laws—that works authored by U.S. government

employees in the performance of their duties are not subject to copyright, making the published PDFs eligible for posting regardless of the publisher's policy. UNL is a land-grant institution with numerous associated U.S. Department of Agriculture centers.

- We recruited entire publication backlists from publishing organizations that lacked serviceable hosting platforms.
- We digitized out-of-copyright materials with special historical relevance to the university, such as works by Roscoe Pound, Louise Pound, Charles Bessey, and others.
- We proactively explore the lists of the publishers who allow posting of their PDFs, and when we find articles by a UNL faculty member we approach that person by e-mail, saying "We have recently seen your article. May we have your permission to archive it and any other eligible ones? And do you have a publication list you could send?" The positive response rate from this approach is close to 90 percent, making it by far the most effective recruitment method we have yet found.

In short, where I had managed to add about 2,400 articles, the help provided by the work-study students (and the pressure to keep them busy) made it possible to add over 6,000 articles in the second year and more than 7,000 articles the third year. We have never done any batch uploads—all content has been added "brick by brick."

So much for the story, in abbreviated form, of our growth from nothing into the (currently) third largest IR in the United States. With that out of the way, let me just try to address some of the issues covered in the previous chapters.

Staffing and Budget

The first year we had a staff of one, but I was full-time and devoted exclusively to the IR (apart from serving on two committees and providing general copyright advice for the campus). We currently have a staff of 1.5, plus three work-study students working ten hours/week each during the academic year. Two of the students do scanning and PDF file preparation, and the other does uploading. After the federal share of their work-study wages, they cost the library about $15 to $20 per week, each.

The Digital Commons package is billed as a flat annual fee, based on full-time employees. The pricing is confidential, but its cost is less than the salary of one entry-level programmer or technician.

Platform

We are enthusiastic proponents of bepress' Digital Commons package. Its greatest advantage is that it allows us to spend almost 100 percent of our time in recruiting and developing content. It worked from the moment it was installed (by bepress) and is almost never down. The annual fee includes customer support, maintenance, and unlimited server space; there is zero load on our information technology department or Web developers. UNL owns the content files and can take them with us if we should come to a parting of ways.

The monthly download reports to authors generated automatically by the Digital Commons system are an extremely effective reselling and recruitment device. This provides feedback to authors that they do not get from journal publishers, and many are astonished at the interest their work receives. Reports available to administrators include numbers of downloads, cover page hits, and referring domains and countries—all of which contributes to a sense of worldwide involvement in the program.

Policies and Preservation

Most of our policies were adopted from those suggested by bepress. We have made some refinements or clarifications:

- Any coauthor may authorize an article's deposit; but any coauthor may request its removal.
- We do not deposit articles *in copyright* without permission of an author or of the copyright holder.
- Depositors should have some connection to UNL; but "connection" is interpreted as broadly as possible.
- UNL Libraries is committed to maintaining its archive permanently and to migrating file formats should need and general practice require.

Marketing and Recruitment

Self-archiving is a wonderful concept, but it does not appeal to most faculty, at least not enough for them to practice it. I essentially abandoned it as a marketing message after about three months. A few authors have made sporadic attempts at archiving their own papers, and I encourage those who want to try, but I also find that checking (and often correcting) the self-archived articles is more time-consuming than gathering and preparing them myself and giving them to a student to upload.

I began with the assumption that younger faculty would be the most likely audience and most enthusiastic users, but the reverse has turned out to be the case. Older faculty with long publication lists are better candidates than younger ones, and the emeriti faculty often turn out to be the best of all.

A wise strategy is to find partners who have large amounts of digital or digitizable content. Without sufficient staff and equipment, it is advisable to become the host, not the digitizer. The Lester Larsen Tractor Test and Power Museum at UNL had a roomful of file cabinets stuffed with technical tractor test reports going back to 1920. They acquired a desktop scanner and used museum volunteers to digitize and upload the entire set, over 2,250 reports. This has now become our largest and most popular series (http://digitalcommons.unl.edu/tractormuseumlit).

Finally (and despite the cliché), it is necessary to think outside the box. It is important not to stop at the campus border—much of our content comes from places other than traditional academic departments: museums, research institutes, U.S. Department of Agriculture–affiliated centers, extension offices, etc. We have never turned down anyone who was interested in participating. Moreover, it is counterproductive to be afraid to "push the envelope"—to take a reasonable chance or a calculated risk: in the online environment, something can always be easily and quickly taken down if it proves a problem (a luxury that print publishers don't have).

Collection Development

Organization of the repository matters more to depositors than to users, most of whom (about 75 percent) reach their destination via Google searches. In some areas we have set up series specific to individual authors; in others we have a more minimal division of (1) faculty publications, (2) dissertations and student research, and (3) department materials (newsletters, program reviews, etc.). A series with only one or two papers can look rather sad and lonely, but one with several thousand papers can be unwieldy both in presentation and for technical management.

Usage

I think the best way to build usage is to assemble a large collection. Online content has a gravity-like property—its attraction increases exponentially with its mass. Of course, the best articles are not necessarily the ones that attract the most usage. Furthermore, usage has very little to do with recentness and everything to do with relevance to common searches. Intriguingly, online bibliographies and open access dissertations seem to be far more popular than their print counterparts.

Some ways we have found to build usage include cataloging book-length works in our online catalog (which also places them in WorldCat), listing them with the Online Books Page (http://onlinebooks.library.upenn.edu), placing links in relevant Wikipedia articles (but see http://en.wikipedia.org/wiki/Wikipedia:External_links), and listing or linking them in appropriate subject-based Web sites. Overall, I think usage is facilitated by posting articles with full-length and keyword-rich abstracts: it helps search engines find them and encourages finders to go ahead and download the article.

My best advice is "Don't wait." Start gathering and posting something as soon as possible. I try not to let a day go by without posting *something*. One thing will lead to another, and that to another, and so on. Waiting for just the right time or just the right content seems pointless; upload what you can get, and go on to the next thing—the browsing public on the Internet will decide what it wants, and, out of those billion people, the odds are most things will be of interest to someone.

Suggested Readings

Royster, Paul. 2007. "The Institutional Repository at the University of Nebraska–Lincoln: Its First Year of Operations." *OCLC Systems & Services: International Digital Library Perspectives* 23, no. 2 (Spring): 183–189. Available: http://digitalcommons.unl.edu/libraryscience/58 (accessed July 19, 2009).

Royster, Paul. 2008. "Publishing Original Content in an Institutional Repository." *Serials Review* 34, no. 1: 27–30; special issue on "Open Access Revisited." doi:10.1016/j.serrev.2007.12.002. Open access preprint available: http://digitalcommons.unl.edu/libraryscience/126 (accessed July 19, 2009).

Royster, Paul. "How to Fill Your Institutional Repository, or, Practical Lessons I Learned by Doing." American Library Association Convention, Anaheim, CA, June 30, 2008. Available: http://digitalcommons.unl.edu/library_talks/40 (accessed July 19, 2009).

Royster, Paul. "Research Showcase: UNL's Institutional Repository." American Library Association Convention, Anaheim, CA, June 30, 2008. Available: http://digitalcommons.unl.edu/library_talks/41 (accessed July 19, 2009).

Royster, Paul. "Value Added Services: Publishing Continuum at the University of Nebraska–Lincoln." (with Joan Giesecke). SPARC Digital Repositories Conference, Renaissance Harborplace, Baltimore, MD, November 17, 2008. Available: http://digitalcommons.unl.edu/library_talks/46 (accessed July 19, 2009) or www.arl.org/sparc/meetings/ir08/valueadded.shtml (with audio; accessed July 19, 2009).

Index

A

B

C

D

E

About the Author and Contributors

Jonathan Nabe has implemented and served as the coordinator of institutional repositories at Southern Illinois University–Carbondale and the University of Connecticut. He is currently the Collection Development Librarian for Science and Technology at SIUC. He has held positions at Brandeis University and SUNY Stony Brook. Nabe has also worked for the Forest Service and the National Marine Fisheries Service. He holds a BS in Zoology from SIUC and an MSLIS from the University of Illinois.

* * *

Suzanne Cohen is the Collection Development Librarian at the Martin P. Catherwood Library, ILR School, Cornell University. She previously served as the Library's Reference Services Coordinator, and she has been involved with the development of an institutional repository since 2002.

James DelRosso is the Web and Digital Project Manager at the Martin P. Catherwood Library, ILR School, Cornell University. He manages the ILR School's institutional repository, DigitalCommons@ILR.

Teresa Fishel has been at Macalester College since 1985 and Library Director since 1997. Prior to becoming Library Director, Ms. Fishel was Head of Reference at Macalester. As Library Director, she manages the library, media services, and campus Web services. Ms. Fishel coordinated the development of the campus Digital Assets Management working group that began in 2004 and oversees the implementation and development of systems to manage digital resources, including images, media, and text materials.

Joan L. Heath is the Assistant Vice President, University Library at Texas State University–San Marcos, having previously served as the Head Acquisitions Librarian. She earned a BA in Journalism and an MLS from the University of Michigan. Ms. Heath has held numerous positions in local, state, and national library associations. She currently chairs the TexShare Advisory Board and is a member of the Executive Boards of the Texas Library Association and the San Marcos Public Library.

Mary Newhart is the Assistant Director for the Scheinman Institute on Conflict Resolution, a joint program of the Cornell University's ILR School and Law School. She is the former Web and Digital Project Manager for the Martin P. Catherwood Library, ILR School.

Dawn Paschal is Coordinator for Digital Repositories Services at Colorado State University, Fort Collins. Her published works include the *Zaire* and *Mali* volumes in the World Bibliographical Series and the *Handbook of Native American Mythology* in the Handbooks of World Mythology Series, all published by ABC-CLIO.

Todd C. Peters is the Head of the Computer Information Services Department at Texas State University–San Marcos. He holds an MLIS and a BA degree in Microbiology from the University of Texas at Austin. He currently serves as Chair of the Texas Library Association's Automation and Technology Round Table. He previously served a six-year term on the TexShare Electronic Information Working Group.

Paul Royster is Coordinator of Scholarly Communications for the University of Nebraska–Lincoln Libraries and manager of the UNL Digital Commons institutional repository. He holds an MA in American Studies from the University of Michigan and a PhD in English from Columbia University. He has been director of the University of Nebraska Press, production manager at Yale University Press, project editor with Barron's Educational Series, and chief financial officer for The Library of America.

Sarah L. Shreeves is the Coordinator for the Illinois Digital Environment for Access to Learning and Scholarship (IDEALS), the set of services and collections that comprise the institutional repository at the University of Illinois at Urbana–Champaign (UIUC). In her position, Ms. Shreeves is responsible for working with faculty, students, and researchers on a range of scholarly communication issues, including author rights, open access, and data curation. She has spoken and published on scholarly communication issues related to institutional repositories as well as the social and technical obstacles to metadata interoperability. She has a BA in Medieval Studies from Bryn Mawr College, an MA in Children's Literature from Simmons College, and an MS in Library and Information Science from UIUC.

Janet Sietmann has been the Reserves Supervisor for Macalester College since 1990 and was instrumental in implementing electronic reserves in 1996. In 2005, Janet added the responsibilities of managing the Digital Commons. She has been instrumental in coordinating the addition of over 140 honors projects, acquiring new journals, and facilitating the digitization of the college alumni publications along with the publications of the Institute of Global Citizenship. She is currently a member of the Digital Assets Management group and the Scholarly Publishing committee that was formed in 2008, as well as other library-related committees.

About the Author and Contributors

Johann van Reenen is the Associate Dean for Research, Science and International Initiatives at the University Libraries at University of New Mexico. He is a Professor of Librarianship and Adjunct Professor of Computer Engineering at UNM. He has more than 55 publications, including four monographs and proceedings and six chapters in books. Recent research and grant topics include enhancing communication and knowledge discovery among karst scientists, collaborative workspaces for analyzing and annotating scientific data sets, the future of science and technology collection development, the benefits of and systems providing open access, Web-based enabling of education and research, distributed learning objects and metadata harvesting, and a 12-year project on consortial support for digital library initiatives and information technology manpower development in Latin America. He currently is Principal Investigator (PI) and co-PI, respectively, on two large grants, the Latin American Knowledge Harvester and IDEC: the Imagery Data Extraction Collaborative.